LIFE-CHANGING HOMES

Kirsten Dirksen

Nicolás Boullosa

LIFE-CHANGING HOMES

Eco-Friendly Designs
That Promote Well-Being

ABRAMS, NEW YORK

CONTENTS

"But there are some whose visions of home are much more expansive. For these dreamers, homes can be a vehicle for our well-being, a shaper of thoughts and experiences, a driver of moments."

INTRODUCTION

When we dream of our ideal home we dream in pictures. Cozy, charmingly cramped interiors, grandma-style, or diaphanous, inside-out sunrooms like Edward Hopper paintings. Snapshots of a white picket fence, a gabled roof, walk-in closets. Once materialized, our homes often too quickly turn into real estate: vessels of investment or showpieces of status. But there are some whose visions of home are much more expansive. For these dreamers, a home can be a vehicle for our well-being, a shaper of thoughts and experiences, a driver of moments. When we add experience to it, a space grows meaningful: We nurture it with our point of view. Home, then, is to a building what duration is to time. (Just in the same way that time can be measured by machines, but its duration belongs to us.)

Early this century, Kirsten and I began to notice—sometimes in extraordinary places, sometimes in conventional settings—people able to dream in four dimensions, whose blueprints of home include the passage of time. People who, by planning for the element of lived experience, had created homes that were able to help sculpt a meaningful life. These were the misfits who had discovered that, often, so-called dream houses could actually get in the way of one's dreams, that the architecture of physical space can impact the architecture of the mind. Just as one aspires to have a house with a garden, one aims at furnishing one's mind and also

OPPOSITE
"Just do your thing," directed Ethan James Green, "but just look at the camera." We were rocking on a half-boat/half-truck on a humid July afternoon in the Far Rockaway Marina (Queens, New York City). Image by Ethan James Green (*Vanity Fair*, November 2019 issue).

> *"When a home is nurtured, it transforms into a sound hearth, a household ready for life's challenges."*

> *"Ours is not really a story of houses; it's always been a search for meaning from our perspective and those of the people we film, and for meaning that is often delivered when people fall into sync with their place."*

OPPOSITE ABOVE
Do buildings sing? In Charles Bello's home amid California redwoods, angles soften into curves, and masonry patterns unfold like melodies inspired by nature.

OPPOSITE CENTER
We've visited many low-tech homes but also pioneering "houses of the future" that often display outlandish concepts, like this rotating house.

OPPOSITE BELOW
Home design profoundly impacts our mood, health, and children's development regardless of budget. Like people, homes can age gracefully—and improve over time.

at cultivating it—home and garden metaphors go hand in hand with fulfillment. Nurture one and you nurture the other. And when a home is nurtured, it transforms into a sound hearth, a household ready for life's challenges.

Our journey officially began in the early 2000s with the birth of *faircompanies, our website inspired by, among other things, Stewart Brand's 1968 decree in the first *Whole Earth Catalog* that "we are as gods and might as well get good at it," which proclaimed "the power of the individual to conduct his own education, find his own inspiration, shape his own environment, and share his adventure with whoever is interested." In retrospect, things that seem obvious now were not that popular just a few years ago. Few cared about eco-pragmatism before Steve Jobs mentioned the *Whole Earth Catalog* in a viral commencement speech. Nobody thought of home as a stepping stone for purposeful experience—though "ecology" is a word that blends two ancient Greek nouns meaning "home" and "principles." And who documented camper-van experiences before influencers?

Once, before "vanlife" was a hashtag, we bought an air-cooled campervan from an old, oddly young-looking, raw-garlic-eating surfer (both owner and engine turned out to be well-maintained) and took off with our three young kids on a quest to discover how little one needed to maintain a sense of home. The vehicle insisted we conform to it to fit the moment—beds down for sleep, kitchen open to eating—and quickly we all, old machine included, seemed to be one organism. Committed to making it work, we settled into routines that landed us in a long present: nice meals, conversations while driving, and nights spent listening to the sounds of our three children's sleep, the steady cadence of each one telling their age. Soon we felt hyperaware of space and time, wondering if this is what it felt like to "be in the moment."

People watch our videos and think we live in a van or off-grid some-where homeschooling our kids. They also wonder: What is our favorite house of all we've filmed? What kind of house should they build? What house would make them most happy? The bloggers and mainstream media who ask us these same questions often seem intent on turning a home into a photograph, reducing a shelter to that snapshot when the sun sets behind the off-grid compound, or when the bikini-clad girl strikes the yoga pose atop her van. Ours is not really a story of houses; it's always been a search for meaning from our perspective and those of the people we film, and for meaning that is often delivered when people fall into sync with their place.

Before the calls from *Good Morning America* wanting to talk about our viral video, or from the *New York Times* asking how we fit into the tiny-house movement, we were living on savings in an edgy part of Barcelona, worried that the institutions of our former professional lives (television and journalism) were weakening and that freelancing was getting more precarious. What people see now in the tiny-house space or the renovation shows wasn't there yet. This was before YouTube was a way of making money, and we were living in a small apartment with no income, posting videos on topics not yet trendy, because we were on a personal search for a better way of living. It was a good life for us, but definitely not the cool thing kids felt worth trying.

Before we met, Kirsten was set to be a cookie-cutter story of American prefabricated success. Raised in still-affordable Silicon Valley and educated in economics at Harvard, she made a postgraduation swerve from finance to working as a secretary at a San Francisco TV station (despite the chorus of family friends: You went to Harvard and you're making five dollars an hour?). She went on to work at national networks, but usually on the fringes (cable networks like Oxygen, Sundance, or MTV). I was seven years younger than her, a Barcelona journalist a bit too aware of Beat Generation writers and not yet ready to spot the cliché of trying to imitate what had once been subversive. Our backgrounds were different but complementary: I was from a place where people counted each other's generations back to their village of origin, whereas her parents had begun their house-flipping careers by moving the family into a motel for most of 1973 to save for a down payment.

When we met, Kirsten was searching for happiness; I didn't think happiness was a thing. We connected because we both wanted something other than what we had seen growing up. We both liked interesting, natural, spiritual places, but we also loved the rich contradictions of modernity and cities, so we began to uncover others who believed there's another way to build a home.

These are the people who helped us reflect on our own definitions of "home," "place," and "belonging." They are misfits, like Al Schwarz (page 140), the veteran computer engineer who fled New York and settled in rural Texas, where he built a stone-covered dome home that saves electricity and protects him (and his neighbors) from the elements when the weather gets rough outside.

These are the ones who renounce modern conveniences, like John and Ruth Maynard (page 51), who rebuilt—log by log—a nineteenth-century cabin on their Long Prairie, Minnesota, homestead. When we asked about the inconvenience of walking to the outhouse in below-freezing weather, John questioned our premise: "You have to put your coat on and get cold, but it's good for the soul. Perhaps we've convenienced our real life away." They are the outsiders who hand-crank their flour, apple

"We were on a personal search for a better way of living."

"... so we began to uncover others who believed there's another way to build a home."

cider, and laundry and believe that some of what makes life worth living lies in the mundane.

Over the past fifteen years, we've performed our own experiments in 4D living: feeling the thrill of arrival after forty-five minutes of near-dark kayaking to reach our beds in a floating cabin on a Canadian lake, or watching the children search for wild fruit and start a fire with flint before overnighting in the absolute quiet of earthen charcoaling huts in rural Sweden. We also want to celebrate the conventional stories of our society, like finishing a long ride on a US highway to arrive, exhausted, in a roadside motel, with our fifteen-, thirteen-, and ten-year-old children sprawled three to a bed.

In this book, we will visit some of these living homes, often overlooked by social media or architecture magazines, where residents embrace the passage of time and the routines of daily life, and, in return for treating their shelter not as an end but as part of the process of living, are gifted with a sense of well-being—a sense of Meaning, with a capital *M*.

—Kirsten Dirksen and Nicolás Boullosa

1. SIMPLICITY

Henry David Thoreau once said, "Our life is frittered away by detail. An honest man has hardly need to count more than his ten fingers, or in extreme cases he may add his ten toes, and lump the rest. Simplicity, simplicity, simplicity! I say, let your affairs be as two or three, and not a hundred or a thousand."

By trying to answer the question of where to live and what to live for, author and philosopher Thoreau refused to conform to what the society of his time expected from him and decided to explore reality on his own terms. His musings as he walked in solitude or with others around Walden Pond still resonate today. By working temporary jobs that would provide what he needed to live for an entire year, Thoreau was able to build a lakeside cabin and explore the relationship between nature and spirituality. He knew that a dream home does not equal a pile of stuff. Today, exposed to abundance and distraction at a much bigger scale, the people in this chapter are exploring the same questions that Thoreau left open, wondering whether the design of a house can make a difference in the way we live and see the world.

W hen BJ and Danielle Siegel talked about building their "dream home" in Sonoma County, they knew the oaks on the rolling hills—and the views of the valley they visited on several consecutive hiking weekends—marked the spot they had been looking for. After they bought a lot on a dirt road, BJ (then senior design director for real estate at Apple) returned with Danielle and their teenage son Jules to camp in different sites on the land. On one of those evenings, as it was getting late, in their search for a place to set their camping tent, they found a stretch of flat land sheltered by oaks on an otherwise steep slope, perched over the valley and protected from the sun and wind. A few weeks later, they built the first structure on their property on that spot: a shed to store camping essentials.

The surrounding trees framed the views while sheltering their tent, and the family set out to build as unobtrusively as possible amid the oaks and rocky terrain. We visited the Siegels there one summer morning. We knew we wouldn't find a big gate or an impressive house upon a hill, but something that blended with the golden, earthy colors the landscape took on during the dry months. "Sometimes, when people build, they want to express all the cool things they can get into a house, and for us, it was kind of the opposite," explained BJ. "We wanted to do as little as possible and make it a comfortable place to live."

As the person leading store design for Apple, Siegel had talked about simplicity in meetings attended by Steve Job. We were reminded of Jobs when BJ described how he cherished focus—and how easy it is to compromise it. To avoid the need to babysit the project while it was being built, BJ came up with the idea of using a prefab house that could be designed remotely and finished at a nearby factory to avoid as many uncertainties in cost, impact, and execution as possible. He worked with Geoffrey Warner, an architect from Minnesota, to create a custom version of Warner's weeHouse prefab.

The result sat light on the land amid the trees: two casually placed, simple cuboids with facade walls of sheer windows. Beyond the living area on the bigger cuboid unit, a balcony cantilevered over the valley.

"I think a lot of people don't necessarily buy into the idea of less is more," BJ said. "I think a lot of people think more is more. And they add

PREVIOUS PAGE AND OPPOSITE: An experiment in cuboid living: The bold, simple design of BJ and Danielle Siegel's Corten steel-clad home blurs the boundaries between outdoors and indoors.

features, and they add complexity, and they add size, and it makes them feel like they've actually gotten more. I think it's much more difficult and much harder to actually get there through doing less. That's the fun challenge." The "less is more" ethos seems to work only in theory: When offered convenience, some of us seem to prefer to buy extra, to get the bigger thing just in case, to accumulate nonessential stuff just for the sake of being able to buy it—maybe taking advantage of a rebate, or a sale marketed as an opportunity.

Before we said goodbye, BJ expressed his concerns about the lack of good affordable housing, especially in places like California. Sometime later, we learned he had left Apple to join a construction startup. (When Kirsten edited and posted our video interview with the Siegels on her popular YouTube channel, one viewer replied with a comment that made us smile: Regarding the architect's care for simplicity, the commenter said, he must have been part of the decision by Apple to get rid of the button on the then recently launched iPhone.)

ABOVE
The Siegels camped on their property for months to place their house in sync with the terrain, trees, and vistas.

"Sometimes, when people build, they want to express all the cool things they can get into a house, and for us, it was kind of the opposite. We wanted to do as little as possible and make it a comfortable place to live."

ABOVE AND BELOW
"I always feel great architecture is like a really great poem," explained BJ Siegel.

Instead of reinventing the wheel, the couple chose a customizable prefab to minimize unknowns and environmental impact.

"My theory is that we had nothing there, so I became obsessed with little things."

Unlike Ralph Waldo Emerson, who lamented the apparent "lack of ambition" in the young Thoreau, the latter decided to explore the essentials of reality from a personal experience that celebrated the need for simplification. Emerson had not understood that Thoreau was ready to sacrifice his social prestige and the perception others had of him to focus on the essentials: "As for work," Thoreau wrote, "we haven't any of any consequence. We have Saint Vitus' dance, and cannot possibly keep our heads still."

Thoreau believed that by keeping themselves artificially busy, surrounded by possessions and spaces too big, too expensive, or too precious to adapt to personal needs and scale, people were pawning their time and losing the opportunity to explore all the possibilities of life. The perception of beauty and the ability to find awe in the simple things around us, he thought, was not compatible with around-the-clock activity. If Thoreau's life project of self-education didn't appear ambitious, by exploring the meaning of a fulfilled life in simplicity and writing about it, he accomplished more than any other "busy" and conventionally successful citizen of his generation.

Seattle architect George Suyama saw in simplicity a path to build the tiny home he had long envisioned. An early life in a Japanese internment camp in Minidoka, Idaho, left many scars, but may also have inspired his love for simplicity: "My theory is that we had nothing there, so I became obsessed with little things. They were long shed buildings; I don't know how many families lived in them. You had one window and a stove area, and there were curtains that separated one

ABOVE AND OPPOSITE ABOVE
Junsei House expresses the very essence of Suyama's architecture as an adult: his instinctual care for simplicity.

OPPOSITE BELOW
Inspired by his previous home, a 500-square-foot (46 sq m) fishing shack in West Seattle, George Suyama designed an 18-foot-wide (5 m) structure with a view of the surrounding trees.

family from another. Maybe it's because there was nothing there that I wanted to make everything as simple as I could."

As an adult, George never experienced difficulties in making things work, no matter how small or devoid of things a space was. He and his wife had been living for five years in a 500-square-foot (46 sq m) fishing shack in West Seattle when the opportunity arrived to buy the narrow lot next door. Determined to celebrate simplicity, the Suyamas built an 18-foot-wide (5 m) home that preserved all the trees on the lot. Interested in the flow of spaces, George designed a structure in which all elements are one color, except for a white box enclosing the service elements: kitchen, bathroom, stairs, and bedroom. Instead of becoming a prisoner of his childhood, George learned to turn the negativity of internment into the liberation of simplicity, a lesson that was hidden in the camp for him to uncover. In his work, life affirmation resides everywhere.

George designed a structure in which all elements are one color, except for a white box enclosing the service elements: kitchen, bathroom, stairs, and bedroom.

LEFT
Suyama's choice of simplicity comes with deep knowledge.

W e tend to see things through the lens of our time, and it's often difficult to spot the difference between important trends and mere zeitgeist noise. The need to create a small place for solitary pursuits already existed before the coronavirus pandemic. Architect James Cutler grew up in rural Pennsylvania at a time when curious kids learned to fix old engines and machines out of rusty parts sitting in yards. Decades later, he still likes to search for authenticity in materials, space, and place, living in an old wooden house he bought and renovated on the forested island of Bainbridge outside Seattle. When we met James, he was dressed in jeans, bearded and long-haired due to the disruption during the early months of the pandemic. While he has designed big corporate and residential buildings, including a home for Bill Gates, he enjoys challenges that bring him back to the basics of building design and its integration in place and time.

As we talked, we marveled at the wild vegetation of the Pacific Northwest that we could see beyond the Cutler's backyard, perched on a fern-covered cliff with views of a sparkling bay. A tree had recently

"There are things that land will accept and other things it will not accept and stay whole."

died at the very center of the yard. James had thought about completely removing the dead tree but ended up keeping its stump when he realized that a little branch had sprouted at its base; an indentation in the stump's surface drained moisture and rainwater down to the young branch. The dead tree was now a piece of art, and maybe a little more.

James had renovated the old house they bought when they first moved to Bainbridge Island, but it was the process of building a "dream bunk cabin" that he codesigned and constructed by hand with his teenage daughter that condensed what he had learned over the years. "Everything in this world has a nature—institutions, people, places," he said. "There are things that land will accept and other things it will not accept and stay whole. The bottom line is, I felt that our job—once we decided to work with the nature of things—was [to understand that] those things take on a will. And our job is to reveal that will, that spirit, and amplify it if we can."

The bunk cabin needed to be as big as a toolshed, with a big front window overlooking the yard and the bay, surrounded by vegetation on the sides for privacy and an inner, transcendentalist blend with nature. James and his daughter spent eight months building the cabin by hand, doing everything from pouring the concrete foundation (in an area known for moisture) to handpicking and rough-sawing planks of Douglas fir. The 8-by-10-foot (2.5 by 3 m) cabin is now the architect's favorite place to work and read, but it is also where he plays cards with his longtime buddies and where his daughter hosts friends to spend the night. All mechanisms within the cabin are meant to be used and share the ethos James developed from his days tinkering with old engines and furniture in his childhood. Bunks hold weight but can be easily moved out of the way; a stove keeps the place warm; and the small "living" area can be arranged for work, study, contemplation, or a moment of relaxation with some friends. Standing at the door of his humble building, James Cutler hardly looks like the type of man who would have designed Bill Gates's 66,000-square-foot (6,100 sq m) house, or Portland's federal building. But to him, the little cabin was no less challenging for being smaller, humbler, and devoid of unnecessary gimmicks.

OPPOSITE
An intergenerational project: By self-building a small structure that requires greater precision and simplicity, James Cutler accomplished the project's main goal—to get to know the cabin's co-builder and co-designer, his teenage daughter, better.

LEFT
On the elegance of simplicity.
A rainwater-catching system
permits gravity-fed outdoor
showers.

S hifting from the Pacific Northwest to the Great Lakes, and from father and daughter to father and son, we contacted architect William Yudchitz to visit the CNC-cut cabin he had built with his son Daniel on their Wisconsin property near Bayfield, a forested area overlooking Lake Superior. We were immediately struck by Bill's hospitality when he insisted on us spending the night in their efficient cabin, complete with "kinetic" wooden-clad shutters, while his son stayed in a second, much smaller cabin.

Both structures seemed to be the realization of a long father-and-son conversation. Not only do Bill and Daniel talk to each other with respect and curiosity, but they also seem to complement each other. Both cabins had been built using interlocking structural panels and could be easily disassembled, and the same principles appeared again in the furniture they had designed for the interior, with chairs and tables that turned into sofas and beds.

The big cabin, which included two mezzanine beds on the sides atop the areas containing services (bathroom on one side, kitchen on the other), has a butterfly roof that captures rainwater and geothermal heating. In contrast, the smaller cabin has a deck on top to enjoy the lake views over the tree canopy. A rainwater-catching system on the side allows Daniel to take outdoor showers. Besides the rainwater shower, the small cabin has an outdoor kitchen and contains a composting toilet and a Murphy bed (adapted from an inexpensive kit with hydraulics), as well as several pieces that are put away completely when not in use: a pop-up bathroom, a fold-down dining table, and collapsible chairs that hang Shaker-style.

BELOW
These Wisconsin cabins
employ CNC technology
to create interlocking,
collapsible spaces.

OPPOSITE
The Yudchitzes enjoy inviting friends over to put the versatilty of the two cabins to the test.

ABOVE
The small cabin, designed for Daniel's use, is a narrow and vertical two-story structure with transforming essentials that fold away and a deck on top.

BELOW
Thanks to interlocking panels, the cabins can be disassembled if necessary. The custom chairs and small tables open into sofas and beds.

Inspired by beauty and patina. Nils Holger Moormann converted an abandoned Bavarian housebarn into the headquarters of his industrial design firm.

Our stay with the Yudchitz family involved many conversations, on topics ranging from Catholicism and spirituality to a trip they had made to Switzerland, where they visited Peter Zumthor's little wooden church in Sumvitg, Graubünden: Saint Benedict Chapel. After our visit, our next stop was a plane ride away, in Bavaria.

Aschau im Chiemgau is a picturesque Bavarian town in the district of Rosenheim, with houses clustered around a medieval castle atop a boulder and with distant Alpine views. Right below the castle, celebrated industrial designer Nils Holger Moormann—who dropped out of law school to specialize in woodworking—transformed a derelict Bavarian housebarn into his company's headquarters.

Nils devoted part of his weekend (an entire Sunday) to meet us, despite his shop being closed and his weekend activities several hours away, a gesture we appreciated. He is a renowned industrial designer who decides to whom he will sell his small-batch furniture, and he likes to create simple, memorable, sturdy, repairable stuff. We smiled when he took his keys and tried to scratch the surface of his Volkswagen campervan's custom furniture to prove his point. It was the beginning of a very particular, extremely enriching day with Nils, a master class in best practices, good taste, ingenuity, a bit of healthy irreverence, and a sense of responsibility.

He produces all his designs 24 miles (40 km) from his company's headquarters or, as he puts it, "within a two-hour bike ride." His furniture is contemporary, but his creative world is forged inside the remains of past centuries. As a result, there's timelessness and uniqueness in his designs. We finished the visit inside two little wooden cabins, both with a corner window, Frank Lloyd Wright–style, wondering when we were coming back and with what excuse.

Only we probably won't need an excuse; Nils Holger Moormann had made us feel so welcome. When we left, we struggled to come up with a reference to describe the remarkable day we'd had. Days later, we found this from Emerson: "I awoke this morning with devout thanksgiving for my friends, the old and the new."

Maybe that was the secret of some people, after all, besides their larger-than-life talent: an authentic generosity toward the people they decide to commit to.

ABOVE
This old Bavarian housebarn was transformed into a showroom with internet-free wooden cabins for customers to stay in.

LEFT AND BELOW
Creative work takes place inside a centuries-old place: Nils Holger Moormann's brand has flourished despite the odds—and despite the efficiency-obsessed rhetoric of business schools.

OPPOSITE
Nils Holger Moormann designs the furniture he wants to use himself.

2. SLOW

With the invention of the mechanical clock, bell towers—and later factory buzzers and personal watches—set the pace of our lives, and we lost touch with organic time: no longer waking with the sun, working with the seasons, eating at natural breaks in the day. As scientific time has synchronized our society, it's become increasingly difficult to follow natural rhythms; instead, we've become obsessed with timekeeping, time-saving, and time management. Still, the duration of time remains a subjective part of the human experience. Some moments seem to last an eternity, while long periods pass in an instant. And sometimes, when we feel at ease with play or work, we enter a state of flow in which time seems to fly away. Being patient or slow in a society that has worshiped efficiency and acceleration may appear counterintuitive, but toward the end of the twenty-first century, small movements in food, fashion, and art began to recognize that life, and products, could be better when not bound to the clock. Living at what musicians call the "tempo giusto," or right speed, may take decades to master, but acknowledging that faster isn't always better can bring about a transformation.

To enter the Valles Pasiegos in Northern Spain is to enter a place where, for a thousand years, time has been fixed to the seasons. Since the eleventh century, shepherds (and their families) have told time by the months, periodically moving their homes and flocks in search of greener pastures. When the "clock struck spring," as it were, they would move to wooden (later stone) huts in the mountains. With the arrival of fall, the *pasiegos*, whose name came from the region itself, would return to their village homes with their cows and a winter's ration of hay.

One late winter day, we entered the area by way of the Portilla de Lunada pass. At 4,429 feet (1,350 m), there was no sign of humans or cows, only the dead quiet of a landscape still in hibernation. As we descended into the valley, the roadsides became dotted with stone shepherds' huts, all empty of life for the moment.

We were headed for the home of Laura Álvarez and her partner, Lewis. Laura had left Cantabria, Spain, as a young architect looking for experience and opportunities; she settled in Amsterdam with her own architecture studio, but she kept thinking about the meaning of home. To her, it was the slower lifestyle dictated by the region that made rural valleys such as the evergreen, steep Valles Pasiegos a place worth returning to in order to build an ideal dwelling.

Despite their proximity to the city, the valleys had stayed agrarian, thanks to a series of small towns populated by nomadic shepherds. Locals had endured the rainy and cold weather since time immemorial by living in hybrid housebarns adapted to the place. Knowing this, Laura set out to find a derelict dwelling that a forgotten family would have shared with a few animals (who also provided free "heating").

At first, Laura planned to stay in the house when she visited the area and rent it when she was back in Amsterdam. Then the coronavirus pandemic hit, and Laura and Lewis realized that the building's dreamy location—midway on a hilly slope made up of a few big trees and pastures divided by a mountain creek—made it an ideal place for introspection. They knew it could become a permanent place, a home.

PREVIOUS PAGE
"Behind the conception of Villa Slow lays one question: If time is the greatest luxury, can a properly designed home help us spend our time more meaningfully?"

RIGHT
The same mountain passes in the Cantabrian mountains that awed Roman chroniclers in Antiquity have allowed sheepherders to move their flocks seasonally.

As she undertook the renovation, Laura easily came up with a name for the housebarn made modern: Villa Slow.

As she undertook the renovation, Laura easily came up with a name for the housebarn made modern: Villa Slow. Like the slow food movement, which is as much a triumph of the beauty of local produce and cooking traditions as it is a celebration of an unrushed way of being in the world, slow architecture aims at considering the context, materials, affordability, sustainability, and long-term commitment of buildings, those who inhabit them either temporarily or permanently, and a relationship between neighboring houses—if any—and nature. The name was a perfect fit for a project in which Laura employed the best local wood for furniture and used forest deadwood for heating the house and the outdoor hot tub. It also reflects the slower rhythms of life adopted by these formerly hyper-connected city professionals: chopping wood, cooking outdoors, hiking, and collecting wood for Lewis's furniture workshop.

At first, living at Villa Slow was only temporary, but in late 2021, she and Lewis decided to stay. When we visited them, the day was rainy and muddy. The couple's dog greeted us, as did two wooly donkeys who followed us around. Laura was still running her architecture firm from home, and Lewis had set up a woodworking studio in an empty building across the road; while it was a weekday, no one looked at a watch or a clock.

Like the roots of the word "ecology"—combining the ancient Greek words for "house" and "principles"—slow architecture aims at understanding surroundings, so a house belongs to those who inhabit it, but it also belongs to the landscape and surrounding ecosystem. Perhaps Frank Lloyd Wright said it best: "No house should ever be on a hill or on anything. It should be of the hill. Hill and house should live together, each the happier for the other." Despite its modern use by professionals, Villa Slow keeps talking to the hill on which it sits and the evergreen valley with its mercurial weather.

OPPOSITE ABOVE
Crossing the mountain passes in secondary roads between Castile and Cantabria in Northern Spain.

OPPOSITE CENTER
Life in Amsterdam was good, but something was missing, so architect Laura Álvarez and her partner, Lewis Bailey, decided to make the villa their full-time residence.

OPPOSITE BELOW
In the verdant Cantabrian mountains of Northern Spain, homes used to shelter the area's grass-fed livestock during harsh days.

ABOVE RIGHT
Laura and Lewis are exploring the slower rhythms of life by working on projects increasingly influenced by life in the countryside.

They built Innermost House as a vessel for facilitating self-examination, undisturbed by stuff shouting for their attention.

To Ralph Waldo Emerson, home was a representation of ourselves: "The constant progress of Culture is to a more interior life, to a deeper Home." With this in mind, Diana and Michael Lorence began working on a simple, unelectrified home in the California woods they called the Innermost House. As they explain, their quest for a house that could represent the essentials they were aspiring to had begun twenty years earlier.

Their 144-square-foot (13 sq m) small home lacks the modern comforts we deem necessary, such as electricity, but it delivers the Lorences' essentials for a comfortable life: "a small, concentrated domestic space conceived for the purpose of what Wordsworth called 'plain living and high thinking,'" according to Diana. In the simple redwood cabin in the coastal mountains of Northern California, the only luxuries are a small deck and a stone chimney, but to Diana and Michael, its very simplicity expands its physical dimensions. They built Innermost House as a vessel for facilitating self-examination, undisturbed by stuff shouting for their attention (books take up most of their shelf space). From their home, they peek into the universe.

The Lorences show how the relationship between fulfillment and material goods, or other status markers, is arbitrary, as long as a lack of things is not considered deprivation but a deliberate choice. Without electricity, a refrigerator, or an oven, they live off lots of vegetables, fruits, grains, and nuts. They cook with a cast-iron pot over the fire, which is also their source of hot water, heat, and indirect light. They don't consider themselves living in material deprivation nor are they trying to prove a point to the world.

"I like to live in this simple environment with just what is necessary: a bed, a stove, firewood. Everything is useful."

Enrico Gri was looking for an abandoned housebarn to restore in Italy's Orco Valley, where inhabitants still use the local Piedmontese language when describing farming or construction tasks and techniques. An online search eventually led to a bramble-filled *baita*, or mountain hut, and Enrico began transforming it into something inhabitable. He first tackled tasks that were not structural or wouldn't need permitting, teaming with a local architecture studio to build a livable wooden area in the two-story stone home's upper floor, creating a house within a house.

Enrico's wife, Paola, an art restorer, insisted they leave as much of the original home as possible, including animal mangers, hayloft tools, and an old chestnut door with original wooden hinges. The existing stable had been built into the hill, causing humidity.

Working with a local mason, Enrico and Paola dug out a new room, to be used as a cellar, to separate the hut from the mountain. Using only stones excavated from the site during construction, they built a dry-stone wall (Paola insisted: no cement), so water does get in during heavy storms. But to Enrico, this is part of life on the mountain. "It's not an enemy," he says of the water. "It arrives. It's curious. It comes, looks around, and is free to go."

Enrico spent five years building nearly everything, from the kitchen cupboards to the wooden dining table that doubles as a bed. He was very particular about details, including insisting that wiring shouldn't be evident. "These days, we are overwhelmed by so many inputs; I was trying to be as simple as possible. I like to live in this simple environment with just what is necessary: a bed, a stove, firewood. Everything is useful."

ABOVE
Traditional slab roof of *baitas*, vernacular small dwellings of the Central and Western Alps in Italy and France.

OPPOSITE ABOVE
To preserve the old housebarn while bringing comfort in, Enrico Gri worked with local architecture firm Studioata to build a wooden structure inside, like a "house within a house."

OPPOSITE BELOW
Paradoxically, the internet is helping those willing to reconnect with old ways. Enrico and Paola Gri found a run-down, inexpensive stable in the Italian Alps by searching online and then set out to restore it on a tight budget. It took them five "well-spent" years to do it, primarily by hand.

Four hours east of the Orco area, in the Alpine valley of Sondrio, Alfredo Vanotti has brought two worthless rural buildings back to life, and he has done so by dramatically improving their potential. We met Alfredo years ago on an autumn trip from the Swiss mountains into the lakes north of Milan through the Passo dello Spluga. Alfredo's home, once a ruined stable owned by his grandfather, reflected a strangely fresh blend of craftsmanship and a very personal, (s)low-tech modern design. A skylight and four large windows facing the valley let the outside in.

While Alfredo was explaining how hard it was to make it work as a local young architect with no contacts, his father was helping our children collect chestnuts. At twilight, when we descended to the bottom of the valley and stopped to say farewell, Alfredo's dad came with a bag of apples for the kids. Two years passed before our next visit to Alfredo, this time to see how he had transformed his grandfather's old barn into an elegant home-studio. His professional situation had also improved, though he wanted to preserve a "slow," laid-back hyperlocality. Alpine inspiration had crystallized in the ethos of his style.

LEFT AND ABOVE
When bringing back to life a ruined stable, Alfredo Vanotti seems to have applied Frank Lloyd Wright's principles. In the interior, Alfredo used cement to express a somehow timeless, rough finishing that "shouldn't be smooth, beautiful, precise."

OPPOSITE
Young architect Alfredo
Vanotti couldn't find any
projects after college.
Instead of growing cynical,
he went rogue, transforming
one of his family's worthless
ruins into a bold, timeless
country home that would
change his life forever.

ABOVE
Harmoniously blending
local tradition and modern
design, the stable became
a manifesto on how to
highlight the timeless
elegance of humble raw
materials.

CENTER
Radical, bold simplicity
made of modern materials
in an ancient structure
and landscape: Alfredo
Vanotti has created his own
architectural language.

BELOW
A ruined stable in Italy's
Orobic Alps is now an
experiment in pure cabin
living in an area that inspired
the poets of antiquity.

N ot all homeowners relearning to embrace slowness both in material and non-tangible ways undertake restorations or adaptations of derelict or abandoned rural buildings, such as Villa Slow or Enrico Gri's Alpine housebarn. Nor do they build homes from scratch from a well-defined, coherent ethos, as Diana and Michael Lorence have with Innermost House.

Carlo "Dino" Marchetti, a naturally elegant, middle-aged dentist, bought a property with gorgeous views of the Italian Alps near Morbegno. There was a strange phenomenon on the property, though: The house's seventies-style detached garage had the best views, "almost as if it were a joke," said Dino. So, he turned the former car park into a modern-rustic annex cabin with the help of architects Gianmatteo Romegialli and Erika Gaggia.

The transformation was affordable, original, and memorable: With a light steel frame around the original cement building, they enabled local plants to wrap the home in a second skin of vegetation, while inside they added raw industrial materials to create a rustic-modern kitchen with a sturdy design to ease its continuous, comfortable use.

Facing the Alps, a big window illuminated a sunroom, perfect for potting plants and relaxing. Now the unattractive building that once dominated the garden and views has been consumed by the garden itself. Dino confessed that the garage-turned-cabin now connected better with him and the surroundings than the big home he had bought the property for years prior; the garage was now "home."

LEFT AND ABOVE
When Carlo "Dino" Marchetti bought his steep property, he couldn't believe the detached, useless parking pavilion had the best views of the Alpine valley below. Soon, the garage was turned into a plant-covered dwelling with expansive views.

"The garage-turned-cabin now connected better with him and the surroundings than the big home he had bought the property for years prior; the garage was now 'home.'"

Perched in the picturesque Rhaetian Alps north of Milan, the property's garage featured the best views, "almost like a joke." When we posted the video on the garage conversion into an elegant modern cabin, a commenter stated: "Sitting up there on a foggy day like that with the faint church bell in the distance is my idea of heaven."

For John Maynard, a retired professor who bought and rebuilt a Minnesota settler cabin log by log, the essentials of home involve escaping our modern obsession with convenience. Like the Amish who live near him, he has chosen bygone technology for his cabin as a way of disrupting contemporary life and creating what is, for him, an ideal lifestyle. "Your water isn't taken for granted. When it gets dark, your whole life changes. We wouldn't have gotten that with plumbing and electricity. It's a very nineteenth-century way of living, but throughout my life, I've tried to dig down and find out the why of things. To find a deeper connection than I find in the present moment." Everything is an exploration for John, from pumping water, to lighting a lantern, to a stroll through the woods that border the home. He doesn't completely reject all modern technology—we used email to connect with him—but he chooses to not let things get too convenient in order to stay in touch with what he believes is the more "real" life. As we walked his land, John explained, "When you walk through these woods, you can find traces of an older history. That's important to me because I think it makes me feel real. It's those kinds of explorations that mean something to me. I have a real need to find out what's underneath me. Where it's coming from. Like finding the roots of the tree. That's kind of how I'm put together. I'm definitely not a twenty-first-century person." As for the inconvenience of going to the outhouse—a 100-foot (30 m) walk from the home—on a cold night, Maynard said, "You have to put your coat on and get cold or swat a few mosquitos, but it's good for the soul. Perhaps we've convenienced our real lives away."

OPPOSITE AND ABOVE
John Maynard was living in the house he spent fifteen years building on his Minnesota homestead when he stumbled into something unexpected: bringing back to life, log by log, an 1870s cabin somebody was getting rid of.

Our fear of missing out seems to be the last societal bond, cutting across cohorts and demographics. Is there an antidote for the anxiety driven by professional and personal FOMO? Some think to have found the way—or, better put, they think they've stumbled upon the right time cadence. Austin dweller Gary Zuker doesn't mind giving things the time he thinks they may deserve or require, and he proves his point inside the comfortable, elegant cob home he built for himself in his spare time.

Gary has witnessed lots of changes in the tech sector, and in Austin itself for that matter. He's aware that many things in our lives go asynchronously slow or very, very fast. A computer engineer for the University of Texas, Gary saw middle age coming and aligned his free time with a personal drive to learn other trades. He decided to dream a bit, despite constraints: How about building a weekend home on the cheap and engaging in a bit of manual learning-by-doing? But, to Gary, building the house wasn't the goal but the means to embark on a creative adventure that has enriched his life.

It all started more than three decades ago when he bought a piece of land on a hillside area outside the Texas capital. The area, covered by a canopy of Spanish oak trees overlooking a reservoir, was still affordable, solitary, and underdeveloped—the ideal spot for a self-built, timeless cob home. Only Gary Zuker didn't know anything about construction or natural materials such as stone or cob. In a pre-YouTube world with much less reference content online, he immersed himself in architecture books, one of which resonated at every step: *A Pattern Language* by Christopher Alexander, Sara Ishikawa, and Murray Silverstein. Inspired by the book—full of practical, commonsense advice—and by all the straw-clay cottages and cob buildings he'd seen, he got ready to build.

After asking around, Gary ended up getting support from a local construction expert who helped with the straw and clay mix; an architect friend gave him the needed advice to prepare for framing, stonework, plumbing, and a scissor-truss system of roof support. For three years, Gary immersed himself in the world of DIY construction, experimenting with natural, locally available materials, and with bioclimatism to keep the house cool in summer and warm in winter with little energy. The house ended up costing $25,000, not much more than the mandatory septic system ($15,000).

PREVIOUS PAGE
How do you build a new "old house"? What patterns make a home beautiful, affordable, and cozy? Can we build a dream home ourselves with little to no expertise in construction? It took Austin software programmer Gary Zuker several years to build his, but he now enjoys the heritage cob home he once dreamed about.

ABOVE
In a pre-YouTube world of DIY construction, Gary Zuker immersed himself in any reference book or publication he could find about natural construction.

CENTER
Detail of the entrance door. An enthusiast of Christopher Alexander's seminal work on humane architecture, *A Pattern Language*, Gary Zucker prioritized slow craft, honest materials, hand tools, hierarchy of scale, and old-world metals.

BELOW
Zuker relied on traditional stone, wood, and metalworking to give the spaces of his cob home a timeless texture, as shown in the hearth. To Japanese farmer and philosopher Masanobu Fukuoka, "the simple hearth of the small farm is the true center of the universe."

"It's part of a philosophy—you wait until you get in a context and then you decide, 'Does the window go here? Does the window go there?'" Sometimes, the view is only clear during the process: "That's the way things ought to be built, kind of going with the flow and not committing ahead of time."

Gary acknowledges that there was never a real set of plans: "It's part of a philosophy—you wait until you get in a context and then you decide, 'Does the window go here? Does the window go there?'" Sometimes, the view is only clear during the process: "That's the way things ought to be built, kind of going with the flow and not committing ahead of time."

Over the years since he began building his traditional home, Gary has developed his own patterns. Among them all, he cherishes one: You cannot build something beautiful if your mind is on the clock. "To the homebuilding industry, 'time is money,' and design choices are always made with this in mind," he says. "This pattern is not really about going slow because beauty can also arise from a single stroke . . . but beauty is highly unlikely to happen when you are thinking about time and money."

3. ITINERANCY

What is home, and what does home have to do with the promise of freedom? Is home always bound to a physical dwelling in a fixed place, or can we claim our home as all that makes us feel at ease, no matter where, even in dire circumstances? With the constant promise of a fresh beginning, itinerancy has inspired a way of being in the world to anyone with enough ingenuity to come up with a fitting abode to roam in, from John "Appleseed" Chapman paddling downriver as he planted apple trees to Walt Whitman dignifying the vagrant confronting the open landscape and big sky of North America to Beat Generation writers hopping on trains as hobos and living in the present moment. In embracing itinerancy, they all felt at home.

ew travel through Northeastern Oregon without a destination there, and we had come to the town of Joseph (330 miles [531 km] east of Portland) on a hot summer day in search of a man named Dan Price who lives in a hole in the ground. It had taken us months to locate him online, but when we did, he confirmed that his home was not an Airbnb-friendly "hobbit hole," but a literal hole in the ground, a place he'd created from his love of the land. He'd promised to explain it all once we arrived.

We bypassed the organic grocery and art walk on Joseph's Main Street for Dan's forested property on the outskirts. He didn't have an address since, technically, he didn't have a home, so we relied on a GPS location to guide us there. We parked above a steep slope, overlooking a quick-moving mountain creek 300 or 400 feet (122 m) below, and messaged him that we had arrived.

Within minutes, Dan emerged soundlessly from somewhere in the grassy slope. He is middle-aged, tall, and slender, with the look of somebody constantly engaged in physical activity. On that day he wore wrinkle-free khaki pants, unexpected for someone who has to crawl through his home. Calm, kind, and reserved, he invited us to follow him down a handmade path to the home's entrance. He didn't say much, but our kids—then aged eight, six, and five—immediately felt comfortable in his presence and began to run when they spotted a small door in the hillside.

We had to go on hands and knees to enter his burrow, but it was possible to sit and move around a bit in the two-room space once inside. Dan had gone underground fifteen years before, although this was actually his fifth home on the property, which was owned by a friend who paid him a few hundred dollars per year to caretake. When he first arrived in 1990, he erected a tepee, but when that began to feel too big, he moved into a 9-by-12-foot (3 by 4 m) willow dome hut. But, given his seasonal travel (he spends winters following the surf), he wanted something even more temporary, so he moved into a four-season mountain tent, only to later fall in love with a cedar-shingled beach shack he'd seen in a book, a replica of which he built for himself.

However, Dan never felt completely comfortable in the "square home," as he called it, so when he was robbed (someone entered a skylight and took his photography equipment and computer), he tore down the shack and moved underground.

Dan was once married, and his children are now grown. When his nest was empty, he had decided to live within his means, spending some months by the coast in a campervan. The rest of the year he spent at "home"—an affordable, comfortable shelter he'd built on his friend's property. By the time we visited Dan, he was living the life he wanted for

PREVIOUS SPREAD
Inspired by Huck Finn and river people, Wes Modes (page 62) built a floating home out of scraps, creating utility and beauty out of old fences and a chicken coop.

OPPOSITE ABOVE
Back in 1990, Dan Price was caretaking a home with a $500/month heating bill. The moment had arrived, he thought, to leave the rat race and start over again. Now, when not out surfing, he works on his comic books from his tiny burrow home.

OPPOSITE BELOW
The cozy burrow rents for one hundred dollars per year (in exchange for cleaning downed trees and repairing fences). Inspired by a cedar shingle beach shack he'd once lived in, his 6-by-10-foot (2 by 3 m) underground dwelling is the place he seasonally calls home.

$5,000 a year, all expenses included (from gas and car parts to food and a few unavoidable bills). He wasn't technically homeless, yet only a few "adults" would have recognized his hobbit shelter inside a verdant hill in Joseph, Oregon, as a "house." Dan owned no property or conventional structure, and he had no loan from any bank to pay.

A short walk across the hillside took us to a second underground shelter, a workshop from where Dan printed his art and self-published his comic books, *The Moonlight Chronicles*. His cartoonist signature was a declaration of principles: hoboartist. Nico asked why he'd chosen "hoboartist" to describe himself, and Dan explained that, to him, "hobo" was not a pejorative term. First used in the US West around the 1880s, "hobo" referred to those itinerant workers (mainly men, who could afford to travel more safely, though safety wasn't guaranteed) with no fixed home or address. Hobos would work in exchange for money, accommodation, or even for food, but they wouldn't settle anywhere long enough to call it home. Home was in the outdoors, full of opportunities for redemption and larger-than-life adventures that inspired folk songs as well as the life and literature of Mark Twain or Jack London.

With the time and the means for manual work on the property, Dan takes pleasure in maintaining his structures: an underground home, an underground studio, a composting toilet, a propane-powered river water shower, a pinewood propane sauna. But, above all else, he is the master of his time and uses it to cultivate his own thinking and work on *The Moonlight Chronicles*.

ABOVE LEFT
When visiting this burrow home, our children felt they had entered a magical world. Price has indeed found his idea of magic: He calls it freedom (by avoiding mortgages and expensive rent).

ABOVE RIGHT
Dan Price stewards a friend's meadow; his seasonal underground home is ideal for his creative work as an illustrator.

Dan explained that, to him, "hobo" was not a pejorative term.

Home was in the outdoors, full of opportunities for redemption and larger-than-life adventures.

Dan doesn't ask much of society, and the town tolerates his conscious living choice: When he asked for power, the city allowed a line to be brought down. "They also approved this composting toilet twenty-five years ago," he explained. "So, I'm kind of grandfathered in. And, as you can see, there's no junk cars or piles of trash around. I keep it really pristine so there isn't anyone complaining. If I had trashed the place and people were complaining, they'd probably come and kick me out."

Yet Dan is aware of his luck concerning how he is perceived: He has the looks of a mature man who didn't quite get old yet thanks to an active, adventurous, exciting life full of reading, conceptualizing art, and playing sports in the outdoors. When we met him, we had already talked to materially wealthy people who didn't control their own time or possess the freedom and self-command we sensed in Dan. "I don't want to be an adult," he explained. "I want to go back as I was as a child, where your days are free. That was a magical time for all of us."

We left Dan with the bliss of a fulfilling day and a present from him: some of his *Moonlight Chronicles* comic sagas, as well as a book by Don Wallis on the life of two legendary river hobos, Harlan and Anna Hubbard, who married in 1943, built a shantyboat the following year, and began an eight-year journey down the Ohio and Mississippi rivers as itinerants who controlled their own destiny.

Thanks to Dan, both the Don Wallis book on Hubbard and Hubbard's own book, *Shantyboat in the Bayous*, accompanied us the rest of the summer. Some nights we were so tired we couldn't even finish a couple of pages before falling asleep. Other days, exhausted at twilight, we'd open the book at random to find some pictures documenting the couple's adventure, and a lot of things would make much more sense.

When everything feels accessible by modern travel or information, when one can hop a plane with minimal friction, near and far lose their meaning. To us, travel shouldn't be a utilitarian, point A–to–point B ride. Until recently, traveling had meant first and foremost a mindset, a declaration of love to the world. We've tried to embrace this old promise of travel, and, living in Europe, long summers have become a call to action: lean, pack-and-go trips through the North American landscape. Modernity, with all its excesses, smiles at us; we can travel, and we have the (minimum viable) means. Itinerancy and life on the road feel very different with the security of knowing that a credit card can get you out of any problematic situation, no matter where you are. Things are relatively tight, and we measure every expense. Still, being able to afford transportation and having emergency money and a place to crash at the end of the day are luxuries compared to the lives of those who start in a needy, fragile position. In our travels, we have also committed to document-

ing our endeavors while trying to attune to other cultures' subtleties, a process we learned at home since we, as a family, are at a crossroads between Europe and the Americas. (Somebody once told us we were becoming a "third culture family": a couple from two different countries and cultures forming a family that ends up living in a country culturally foreign to theirs.)

One summer we were crossing the United States from east to west when we met Wes Modes, a Californian who, inspired by Harlan and Anna Hubbard, had built his own shantyboat to revive a forgotten river lifestyle. When we met him, Wes was docked at a transient slip in Knoxville's volunteer landing marina and getting ready to begin a 652-mile (1,049 km) trek down the Tennessee River. As a professor of art at the University of California at Santa Cruz, he had already spent several long summer vacations on the river filming his ongoing online documentary, *A Secret History of American River People*, to capture this "endangered" way of life. Instead of seeing shantyboat dwellers as marginalized, Wes sees their hardships as history with a lowercase *h*, explaining, "It's a form of history that is just as valid and just as legitimate as history with a capital *H*."

ABOVE
A matter of priorities: Instead of craving a middle-aged status symbol, Wes Modes decided to reconnect with the history of American "river people" by sailing down the Mississippi.

OPPOSITE ABOVE
Like poets, writers, and misfits before him, Wes Modes felt the mighty presence of the Mississippi River in the collective unconscious. He hatched a plan to build his own shantyboat from reclaimed materials in his Santa Cruz backyard, then transported it to Minnesota and began a "Huck Finn–style" journey downriver.

OPPOSITE BELOW
The 10-by-8-foot (3 by 2 m) shanty boat packs a lofted bed for two, a compost toilet, and a propane kitchen with a plumbed sink.

Some people must take different sorts of risks when choosing a transient lifestyle. A little time after our visit with Wes, we met Paris and Lovell Lee, US Army veterans who moved into Lovell's retired computer repair van after running into financial trouble while, as they put it, "living a short life of luxury in the Los Angeles Valley." When they were about to move north for college in high-rent San Francisco, they decided to cut costs by giving up any permanent home. They'd road tested the van on short trips with an air mattress but were initially unprepared for a full-time mobile life (and the unending search for legal overnight parking).

By the time we met them, Paris and Lovell were more seasoned after a few years living in the van. They had parked beneath the Golden Gate Bridge for the shoot, but on our arrival they explained it wasn't somewhere they were allowed to spend the night. As the fog rolled in, we tucked into their tiny van where they talked about their dreams of filmmaking (Paris) and fashion design (Lovell). Due to their very limited space, their itinerant lifestyle had forced them to prioritize. There was no space for anything but what would add value to their lives. Their television had been replaced by active toys like a longbow, mountain bikes (tightly mounted at the back "garage"), and cameras for Paris to master her craft. The couple have also started a YouTube channel where they avoid #vanlife cliches (e.g., hyper-orchestrated videos of bikini-clad yoga) and instead try to show reality: getting towed and broken windows.

Undeterred by the less-than-Instagrammable moments, Paris and Lovell have remained on the road. They started tagging their videos #blackvanlife, in hopes of setting an example for others in a non-idealized way. They still haven't achieved complete financial independence, but when we last spoke, they were talking about getting into the stock market.

On the foggy summer day when we met, their van felt very small—though not unfamiliar to them, after their experience in the military—but Paris and Lovell seemed to expand the space with their art: Paris's photography and Lovell's fashion design. As we listened to Lovell sing a pitch-perfect serenade to Paris before we pulled away, we felt the limits of the home drop away.

OPPOSITE ABOVE
Paris and Lovell developed a sense of endurance and an itinerant concept of home in the Army; #vanlife is a way to buy time until they get established in their careers.

OPPOSITE BELOW
Paris and Lovell Lee learned to maximize tiny spaces in the military, so when they started college in San Francisco, they decided to turn their van into their "stealth" home.

More recently, we met Vaughn Dabney through a friend in Los Angeles; he had converted an old, green delivery truck into a combined home/studio. Like Paris and Lovell, Vaughn wants to become a role model for young people growing up in underserved communities, but with his background in computing and start-ups, the mobile home was also a chance to explore his own limits. Using his aptitude for engineering, he built a Murphy bed (sitting on two forty-pound gas struts) that could turn his living room space into a comfortable bedroom in five seconds.

Nearly everything in his home has been engineered; when we commented on the micro-adjustable backrest on his couch, he showed us how he'd used locking shelf brackets, aluminum tubing, L brackets, and a threaded rod for ultimate customization. As he showed us the large mural he'd painted on the back of his bed/wall, Vaughn talked about the freedom he felt to creatively explore without the confines of an expensive LA rent.

Vaughn has begun designing vans for other people; his company is called Unoma Haus, as a celebration of his Nigerian and German roots. *Unoma* means "beautiful" in Igbo and *haus* is the German word for "house." "This is about changing the landscape and changing the narrative, not just of what a home is," explains Dabney, "but also of the people living in dwellings like this. I want to be an example, a safe haven, and a trustworthy figure encouraging people to do this."

ABOVE
Trained as an engineer, Vaughn Dabney wouldn't settle for yet another conventional van conversion despite his lack of construction experience. Used to interdisciplinary challenges, he employed surprising, unconventional workarounds, from magnetic door locks to industrial gas struts for a Murphy bed.

LEFT
"I can get away with stuff that these other [parked RVs] can't, though, because I don't look like an RV. I look like a delivery truck. It's something I didn't even realize would be a thing until I started parking in urban areas."

BELOW
Kirsten to Vaughn: "People think you're delivering."
Vaughn to Kirsten: "People think I'm delivering. I'm delivering happiness."

n 2019, we received our first email from Aaron Fletcher, a nomad who didn't define himself as homeless, but rather "homefree." A dozen years before, Aaron had decided to explore an unusual idea: to become a "guerrilla grazer," roaming from property to property with grazing animals as his only companions. First, he tried with goats but realized sheep were more suited for on-demand grazing, as well as other services he could offer in exchange for a place to sleep, some food, or a bit of money.

It would be two years from that first email before we finally connected with Aaron, when we happened to be passing through Ashland, Oregon, and he was parked for the day on the side of the main road leading into town. He had brought his sheep to a field of shrub brush—with the owner's permission—to graze for the evening. Everything Aaron owns can travel with him: a metal sleeping cart designed by him and a friend; a few precious items used to cook, work, stay safe, and provide food; and a flock of sheep so small, they reminded us of a group of sled dogs. Although Aaron is technically homeless, no one can call him destitute; he has a constant supply of sheep's milk, homemade cheese and kefir, foraged nuts, vegetables, and spices. He also has tech: a smartphone and flexible solar panels. He is living a conscious existence and, if interested, could explore a more conventional lifestyle. Yet he isn't rushing to leave behind his sheep, start a traditional job, rent a place, and try to "reenter" society.

In our own travels, we have come to understand that homelessness is seldom a conscious choice, though some thrive even in extreme situations. Itinerancy is set to maintain its continued relevance to this country's traditions, long chronicled by writers of many genres, including Walt Whitman, who wrote in "Song of Myself," "I tramp a perpetual journey.... My signs are a rain-proof coat, good shoes, and a staff cut from the woods."

OPPOSITE ABOVE
Despite modernity's efforts to judge our worth by our possessions and credit score, Aaron Fletcher's life as a traveling shepherd is a portal to ways of fulfillment detached from conventional housing or money exchange: He offers sheep grazing in exchange for food or places to rest.

OPPOSITE CENTER
"This isn't a weekend prank." Aaron lives in his tiny sheep cart all year, even during the snowy Oregon winter.

OPPOSITE BELOW
Aaron eats foraged foods (wild greens and seeds), and even forages ingredients to make his own toothpaste. He also eats and some traded meat, potatoes, and citrus.

4. IMPERMANENCE

Time goes on, and we don't live forever, but some constant beliefs, hopes, and passions seem to change little over the generations. An old Sumerian proverb says, "Something offered is not offered, something finished is not finished, and nothing changes." The Greek philosopher Heraclitus put it this way: A river may appear constant, but water flows downstream. Like the river, our lives are shaped by continuous, unnoticed transformations.

Similarly, some of the stories referenced in this chapter happened when our children were toddlers, whereas we produced the latest ones while raising three teenagers. By the time this book hits the store, our current favorite jeans will be too old for some (perhaps not for us), and our oldest daughter, Inés, will be getting ready for college. Time goes indeed, and accepting impermanence without wishing things to be different can be a way to fully engage with the present moment and its possibilities.

W e've met a few people who know about rivers. Nowadays, Jérémie Malvy is an accomplished entrepreneur, cherished by the Parisian community he has served with his restaurants and organic grocery cooperative. It wasn't always like that: He arrived penniless in Paris more than twenty years ago, speaking a little English and no French. He spent some rough nights, often sleeping under the Seine bridges. Jérémie recalls talking to the Seine; coming from Pakistan's Punjab province (Punjab means "land of the five waters"), he sensed the river would inspire him to find the strength needed to start a new life. Everything flows, he thought to himself.

Those years are behind him. Are they ever completely gone, though? In recognition of creating local jobs, his Parisian circumscription offered him a river dock permit, which brought him back to the river. So the successful, middle-aged Jérémie Malvy, now a local gentleman fluent in impeccable French, bought an old cargo riverboat for €11,000 and spent two years transforming it into a luminous, two-story modern home. In honor of the river waters he came from, he called his boat the *Panjab* (Punjab) and used every single opportunity on deck and inside to grow several species of ornamental plants that he takes care of personally.

There's an open-plan kitchen and living room on top and private quarters with several bedrooms and bathrooms down below. When we visited the downstairs with Jérémie and his partner, Sara, we could sense Jérémie's pride; he had used materials and textures that blended Parisian sophistication with an Eastern sensibility, like copper and bronze instead of stainless steel for faucets and fixtures, bringing a timeless character to everyday things.

At the end of our visit, as we observed the Seine waters passing by from the lower level of the boat, half-submerged below the water, Jérémie spotted a spider by one of the windows. He delicately found the silk from where the spider was hanging, and, lifting it gently, he helped the creature outside. Then, leaning on the window, he contemplated the water flow like an ancient Eastern philosopher. He was in Paris by the Seine, but he also reflected on the Punjab.

PREVIOUS SPREAD
Jérémie Malvy named his converted cargo boat *Panjab* to honor the river that saw him grow. The Seine makes him feel at home.

ABOVE
With the help of his partner, Sara, Jérémie turned a derelict cargo boat into the two-story house of his dreams.

OPPOSITE BELOW
Jérémie Malvy cares for all the plants onboard, an activity he finds soothing.

A little more than 500 miles (805 km) to the south of Paris, just across the Hendaye border with Spain, young Basque artist and designer Tas Careaga was looking for a place to live and was open to exploring ideas that could align with his work and transient philosophy of life. When he first saw the ruins of a sixteenth-century small church near a Basque hamlet that the local bishopric was selling for little, he decided to go for it. There was one caveat: The new owner was required to rebuild the church respectfully, keeping its external appearance.

Careaga engaged friends and family to clear the ruin of debris and overgrown greenery; then he revamped it into his home. Inside, they preserved the patina of the walls and vaults, leaving the main nave open and placing a wooden frame in the back of a space, to support a double mezzanine: an open bedroom on the second floor and an office perched on the third floor with access to a special introspection nook inside the former bell tower.

The apse now houses a high-ceilinged, unique kitchen with art hanging over the preserved thick walls. It was a church in the past, "but now, it's my *etxea* ('home' in Basque)," explains Careaga, who also installed a skateboard ramp on his home's very special "backyard" perched over a forest.

The enchanting place brought us back to a scene from Anthony Minghella's movie *The English Patient*, when Lieutenant Kip from the British Indian Army shows the protagonist (Hana, a WWII French-Canadian nurse played by Juliette Binoche) the paintings inside a derelict Italian church by lifting her with ropes up and down the apse, while the frescoes are randomly lit up by the torch she holds.

ABOVE
People don't normally buy derelict sixteenth-century churches to turn them into their homes. That didn't deter young Basque artist Tas Careaga.

OPPOSITE
We have seen few houses that display this much character, elegance, and modern allure after a conversion.

ABOVE
Old paint layers and the texture of time add to the place's character. The vaulted apse showcases Tas's eclectic art collection, a blend of inherited old family portraits and his own work.

CENTER
Tas Careaga walks to his open kitchen. To him, the formerly abandoned church has regained a sense and purpose: being one's home.

BELOW
Tas's bedroom on the mezzanine's second floor perches over the building's nave like the vantage point of an artist's dream.

OPPOSITE ABOVE
The church required the owner to renovate respectfully, and Tas was up to the task, adding a new roof and little else outside.

OPPOSITE BELOW
Neighbors were glad to see the small abandoned building come back to life and become Tas' home. (There are six other churches in Sopuerta, Biscay, for a population of 2,569.)

"The idea of being unfinished is fundamental. Houses are there to be lived in. They're there to be personal expressions of people."

As the passing of time leaves its traces, some buildings and places, like some people, seem to have learned the secret of aging well: They didn't find the mystery of the fountain of youth but rather a way to embrace change, so time doesn't leave a scar but a halo of wisdom. Enter Tim Seggerman: He bought his townhome in the Brooklyn neighborhood of Crown Heights at an auction in 1987. It cost him $140,000, and he spent his entire savings on the down payment of $14,000. At that moment, the home had been abandoned for twenty years, and the holes in the roof had begun damaging the structure. A trained builder and master carpenter, Seggerman revived the house while adapting its interior to the changes that came with his family moving in: a lofted bed morphed into an indoor cabin for kids, then became a loft again when no children were staying. The bedroom had also provided an office space for his ex-wife, but after their divorce, the wall came down once more.

It all seemed a part of one of Will Eisner's graphic novel sagas set in the legendary New York City tenements, a testimony of how old buildings preserve their appearance outside, whereas things inside don't remain the same. Though things change, Seggerman wasn't trying to press "pause" and freeze his life in some sort of preretirement fantasy: As an architect and carpenter, he had learned to appreciate the impermanence of things and our limited ability to shape them to our needs, and to embrace the transience of precious moments that feed our experience.

Like the Japanese concept of *wabi-sabi*, which celebrates imperfection, impermanence, and incompleteness, Seggerman's goal isn't closure: "The idea of being unfinished is fundamental. Houses are there to be lived in. They're there to be personal expressions of people. So many architects, you're dealing with fine lines, and everything is precise, insanely precise, but you know that in reality, you get out, and there are so many things that go on. You can build it perfectly. It might look nice today, but you have to allow for life."

OPPOSITE ABOVE
Things were different in New York when you could buy a house in Brooklyn for $140,000 and a down payment of $14,000. Tim Seggerman did so in 1987.

OPPOSITE BELOW
Tim believes in the flow of things. Stuff is never "complete," and the goal isn't closure: "You have to allow for life."

Kirsten's YouTube videos also remind us of the passage of time, a place on the internet where our children keep growing in front of our audience. During a visit to a picturesque little hamlet in the Catalan region of Penedès (not far from our children's grandparents' home one hour southwest of Barcelona), our family stumbled upon a house for sale. It looked uninhabited; the exterior showed a mismatch of attempted budget renovations behind battered cement cladding, contrasting with the manicured village clustered below a twelfth-century castle.

Soon, we embarked on renovating this fixer-upper, which needed serious work. The coronavirus pandemic hit right when we had started and it made the lengthy process even more complex. In those difficult days, our renovation became a solitary process but also a way to reflect on our own fragility facing uncertainty.

We discussed the renovation and our goals, often: Was it going to be a purist attempt at picturesque authenticity, getting rid of most of the old renovations aimed to "improve" the house's old character with little success? Or could we embrace the changes made by former inhabitants? We decided to go with updates of our own while keeping the elements and materials that were in good shape, improving the flow between rooms and floors.

Once the main works were finished, we began our sporadic stays. Routines and lived moments soon allowed our family to call that house our home —a place to celebrate and reflect on our own impermanence.

As life goes by we imagine ourselves like many empty nesters, refusing to fence ourselves off in a home that feels empty and underused: our renovations are the alternative, helping us feel useful and part of society.

ABOVE
As we embarked on our own fixer-upper's renovation, we wondered: Can a dark, cramped home become a luminous flexible home for a young family of five?

OPPOSITE ABOVE
Years back, while visiting Nico's parents, we discovered a cliffside hamlet overlooking a serene reservoir reminiscent of Castel Gandolfo (the hilltop village near Rome where the Pope goes in Summer). Soon after, we began renovating a fixer-upper there.

OPPOSITE BELOW
A small fortress upon a gentle Mediterranean hill. Designed in the Romanesque style, the village's old castle was among the southernmost defense points of the County of Barcelona in early medieval times.

LEFT
Front view of the country home that we restored using natural limestone to plaster the walls, local wood for the window frames, and off-the-shelf materials to complete the structural work.

BELOW
We discovered an old clay arch covered by previous renovations. We were happy to bring it back.

ABOVE
Upstairs, we turned a low attic into an airy room displaying the unspoiled surroundings. We added a Frank Lloyd Wright–like corner window to amplify the effect.

CENTER
The main floor hosts a kitchen and living room where the simple, transformable furniture is set for family gatherings amid the Van Gogh in Arles ambiance (simple wooden furniture and a reinterpretation of the area's timeless rustic wooden chair).

BELOW
Moveable handmade shades of local woven grass (the traditional "esparto") preserve privacy while keeping the interior cool.

OPPOSITE ABOVE
The 380-square-foot
(35 sq m) converted home is
less than a fifth the size of
her former home, but Lee
Reich doesn't miss anything.
Quite the contrary: The
space feels "like a hug."

OPPOSITE BELOW
Lee now has more
opportunities to be with her
family, and they all cherish
their respective privacy,
which the setup provides.

ABOVE
Widower Lee Reich decided
to pool resources with her
daughter and transform
an unused garage into a
charming in-law unit.

W hen Lee Reich's husband died after nearly a lifetime of marriage, she refused to stay at the home they had built together and thought it was time to move closer to her daughter's young family in the Northern California city of Santa Rosa, one hour north of San Francisco. For a while, Lee and her daughter, Stacy Lince, were paying a collective $4,000 per month to rent their separate Santa Rosa homes, but when a fire in the area ruptured their economy, Lee decided to help buy a home with a garage. Respectful of people's privacy and proud of her own, the widow's idea didn't consist of living under the same roof with the Linces: They transformed the garage into a cozy in-law unit instead.

Despite its proximity to the main house, the garage-turned-second home is masterfully private—and luminous. As for her new 380-square-foot (35 sq m) place, "It feels, it is home to me now." It's less than a fifth the size of the home Reich had shared with her husband, but she likes the coziness of the living room with an open kitchen, as well as the spaciousness of the bedroom and bathroom. After purposely downsizing her possessions by giving away books and a king-size bed, she now likes to have her daughter and grandchildren over, "even though we all still enjoy our privacy."

n 2007, Paul Cutting was about to finish college and didn't know what to do next: "Nowhere closer to figuring out the purpose of my life, I stumbled onto something big." It was his fourth year studying in Iowa City when, at home in Decorah for winter break, he found an ad in the local paper. Somebody was giving away an old prairie log house. Paul knew little more about log houses than "Abe Lincoln's unpresuming upbringing." If even the sixteenth American president had been born in a log cabin, why were some people dismissive of their vernacular charm?

Paul went to see the log house the morning after spotting the ad and, feeling its imminent demise, he bought it on the spot for $600. This impulsive action would open a world that had not been apparent until then: The way the logs had been cut and put together traced the construction to a rich but forgotten heritage of Norwegian Americans settling in the Great Plains from the mid-nineteenth century onward.

The process became the archeology of early industrial production, celebrating 150-year-old nails and planks.

As Paul Cutting began to take the log cabin apart meticulously, he documented each piece and nail so he could put it back together in a new location nearby. He grew interested in the lives of those who had built similar homes in the region: "I drove something like 5,000 miles that spring and located a hundred houses." But these houses had not been documented and didn't belong to any registry. Built between 1800 and 1870, "they were vanishing, and nobody seemed to notice."

Cutting rebuilt not one but two settler's log homes on his parents' farm, and in a few years, he bought several homes at a symbolic price, disassembling about a dozen and painstakingly rebuilding them log by log. Among other things, the process became the archeology of early industrial production, celebrating 150-year-old nails and planks. His log house restoration project has provided an education in building handwork, cabinetry, and impermanence that no college can provide with such a hands-on approach and depth. And a school of life.

ABOVE
The "corn Iowa" original
home.

n rural New Jersey, architect Adam Kalkin had a different idea of preserving the area's rich farmhouse heritage. He restored an original clapboard cottage amid the greenery of rolling hills and the spare houses that Philip Roth describes in the novel *American Pastoral*.

It was a bright day when we drove onto the dirt road leading to his house. We spotted a cottage, at the side of which a couple of workers (one of whom was Kalkin) were unloading heavy construction gear and scaffolding from a big truck. We let him finish and entered the property on foot. The main house was in front of us, impossible to miss in its grandiosity. Kalkin had not stopped with the little cottage restoration and had decided to create "kind of a ship in a bottle": Instead of adapting the original limited space of the heritage home, the log house was now the core of a larger dewlling: a Butler airplane hangar on top of the original structure. The result is mesmerizing.

At one end of the hangar, a massive glass serves as his studio window, whereas at the other end of the 27-foot-high (8 m), 33-foot-wide (10 m) space, Kalkin created a grid of nine rooms with chambers on different floors accessible through external stairs.

From the higher-up rooms, we could see both the hangar-house exterior and the center of the enclosed structure, with the open cottage serving as the living core, the "hearth" of the young household. "It's got kind of an urban roof-scape thing; I always like seeing roofs. You get that feeling like you sometimes get in New York.… You know, just because you're in the country—I want to recall urban experiences. Why can't you recall urban experiences in a house in the country?"

Can you turn an airplane hangar into a cozy home that includes an architectural studio, an old cottage, and a contemporary home for a young family? Ask Adam Kalkin.

Adam Kalkin's historic cottage in rural New Jersey is now encased like a dollhouse in a converted hangar, "kind of a ship in a bottle." The result is awe-inspiring—and very livable, it turns out.

ABOVE
One end of the hangar includes a series of chambers with a glass wall and views of the space below.

OPPOSITE BELOW
Kalkin's office is at home with the farmhouse-in-a-hangar home overlooking New Jersey's rolling hills.

Inside, the carcass of a seventeenth-century cottage seems frozen in time after three centuries of aging.

n the spring of 2019, we made the drive through winding secondary roads to a small village in Herefordshire, where the West Midlands meet the hills of Wales.

David Connor, a tall, mature architect in casual but elegant clothing, welcomed us into his house, Croft Lodge. Connor and his wife, Kate Darby, had bought the place with a three-hundred-year-old crumbling cottage on it.

They soon found out they had to preserve the structure or lose any right to build. Instead of restoring the cottage and turning into an idealized interpretation of what had once been, they chose not to repair it but to encase it in a new house that would protect the ruin from the elements. Mirroring the old shape, the new building creates two walls and two roofs where the old cottage still holds, while at other spots, the missing part drops away, and the white shell recreates what it once was.

Connor explained that architecture can reflect the memory of what it once was. From afar, the new home—in black corrugated iron next to a magnificent oak tree on the nearby commons—blends with the farm buildings around. Inside, the carcass of a seventeenth-century cottage seems frozen in time after three centuries of aging with no more protection than the now-crumbling original structure.

There are dry ivy branches, and the trimmings bring an interesting bluntness to the compound. The old cottage's interior is still used and serves as a unique, enchanted scenario for some books and seats, sculptures, and art pieces, most of them by Connor himself. A cast iron stove sits at the old hearth.

We did not know back then, but we would unconsciously place a similar cast iron stove where the old fireplace had sat at our house in Penedès which we renovated after visiting Croft Lodge. The wall also shows the patina of old fires and the scars of several renovations on the sides of the chimney.

5. ELEVATION

What do we seek high up in the mountains? In an interview with the *New York Times* on March 18, 1923, English mountaineer George Mallory was asked, "Why did you want to climb Mount Everest?" To which he responded, "Because it's there." Born in the plains of Massachusetts, Henry David Thoreau proclaimed in 1848 that "only daring and insolent men, perchance, go there." Up there, the strenuous conditions of thin air and isolation are great equalizers. "A few hours' mountain climbing make of a rogue and a saint two fairly equal creatures."

"Tiredness is the shortest path to equality and fraternity—and sleep finally adds to them liberty," wrote German philosopher Nietzsche, who walked tirelessly in the Swiss Alps. In the mountains, social etiquette loses its meaning, and we focus on the essentials. But if visiting the mountains is difficult, how about living there?

t was a mild day in Northern Italy, and we were on a family trip through the Alps, navigating dozens of switchbacks to climb up a forsaken mountainside road had slowed us to a runner's pace. The mood in our car reflected that of modern vacationers far away from easy access to convenience.

We were in the heart of Europe, yet our feeling of isolation, aggravated by potential mechanical issues in our 1989 G-Wagen—which had failed before in the middle of nowhere—made us think of the might of nature—capable of giving and taking everything at once. Our car wasn't electric, but we experienced range anxiety nonetheless since knowing how much gas was in the tank was a guess, especially when the fuel gauge guessed the remaining amount on a slope.

We looked at the dark skies and the eternal snow patches by the side of the road, and nature's solemnity set a mood of sleepy transcendence. The veil of mist made us think of a dream.

We were in these particular mountains because we had received an email from a young theologian named Johannes Schwarz, who, in his message, defined himself as "a priest by trade" fixing up a €20,000 "run-down *rustico*" (farmhouse) high in the Italian Alps. He had decided to turn the little derelict building, the only dwelling in an abandoned, very steep farmstead, into "a habitable hermitage with chapel and all."

Johannes had left his parish "to withdraw for a few years" in the shadow of Monte Viso, known in the Alpine area of Piedmont bordering France as Il Re di Pietra (The Stone King), a colossus he had hiked before. We left the car at the summit and followed him on foot.

When we finally made it up to the mountain pass, Ximena, our second youngest, then twelve, had not listened to her mother's explanations

PREVIOUS SPREAD
Johannes Schwarz: "I'm an Aristotelian of sorts, and the Aristotelian school in Greece was called the *peripatei*, which means the ones who walk around. So, yeah, I can think better when I walk around."

ABOVE LEFT
To be as self-sufficient as possible, Johannes makes his own bread, which he shared with us. For heating and cooking, he built a combination rocket stove and masonry heater by creating his own casts and loam coating.

ABOVE
A view of the humble hermitage, high in the Alps.

RIGHT
Johannes restored the surrounding soil's fertility to grow his own fruit and produce on the steep, terraced hillside.

BELOW AND RIGHT
Johannes' unpretentious
version of paradise on Earth
is a small and steep lot of
land high in the Alps with a
rustic home to restore and a
garden to care for.

about the place we were visiting, which helped in convincing her that the young, kind, energetic man in a black cassock had been introduced as Your Highness (her interpretation of the sound Jo-hannes). The apparent remark made her believe we had entered an enchanted world, a tiny kingdom up in a mountain. As we drove away in the car at the end of the day, she demanded more information about "the sort of prince" we had just visited.

We soon found out Johannes had not exaggerated; his place was an old, small stone farm perched on a forested, steep hillside displaying the wide color range of the fall in a deciduous forest. He had paid €20,000 to reinvigorate house and property, creating a remote Virgilian hermitage his unpretentious version of paradise on Earth.

To ensure self-sufficiency during his sabbatical years building his hermitage homestead for contemplation, Johannes made his own bread and got some of his basic needs off the hilly lot despite the elevation, which brought him to joke about his varieties, "grown at the highest known altitude." Potatoes, leafy greens, and bush and tree fruits. Yet his work terracing the steep hillside was no joke.

Inside, he had used the old barn's two-floor plan to locate the living area around a self-made rocket stove and masonry heater on the ground floor, while the upstairs included his bedroom, a video production studio with gym gear, and access through the old balcony to the room where he built a wooden-arched chapel in the primitivist styles of Byzantine, Lombard Romanesque, and Gothic.

Though inspired by the early Christian hermits who ventured "into the deserts of Egypt and Palestine searching for a more rigorous life," Johannes had revived the decaying *rustico*, filling it with a humble comfort we appreciated as the late-fall sun receded and a blanket of cold reminded us we were high in the Cottian Alps.

The rigor of the mountains attracts the adventurous, the solitary, and those trying to break ground in their disciplines. Hermits, artists, writers, misfits. In the American heartland, Greg Parham was on a quest of his own: scion of a religious family, he tried to find his own call by exploring nature across the Rocky Mountains. His passion for the outdoors prompted him to explore the American West on his mountain bike, but he soon realized that the mountain towns that most appealed to him were just too expensive.

When we visited in July 2020, it was a hot summer day in the picturesque town of Durango, in Southwestern Colorado, where Greg was working on three homes for his company, Rocky Mountain Tiny Houses. Despite the heat, the proximity of the river and his home's tree-covered location made the place pleasant. In front of us, the highest peaks kept their snowcap. We went down to the river with our three children to Greg's workshop, cooled by the water and a few aspens providing shade.

Greg, a young but assertive, bigger-than-life builder, explained that attending college had not brought the expected certainty of finding meaning through work and relationships, but he was sure of one thing: He felt at home in the Rockies. So he moved to Durango and built his first tiny house to afford rent. His build attracted attention from friends and passersby, and a decade later, his company had built more than eighty weather-proven, rugged, "mountain style" tiny homes.

Building affordable, movable tiny homes, often with salvaged local material, had rescued him from a dire situation early on as house prices climbed in desirable ski towns such as Durango. In a few years, he had gone from earning a living from his builds to hiring some help and building himself another home to live in with his fiancée, Stephanie.

They called their tiny house the San Juan. The home felt sturdy and very crafty. Its precise, shingled encasing arches up and out to maximize space inside, which reminded us of a caravel's hull from the Age of Discovery, with its ceiling warping around a central nerve like the organic structure of a leaf. Inside, Greg's care for the small volume of the space was expressed with a mechanical elevator bed and a tabletop that slides into multiple positions with no mechanism other than wax. We were in awe of the design ingenuity.

f Greg Parham had found tranquility and vocation in the Rockies, our family felt at home in the Pyrenees. On our trips back and forth from Paris—where we lived for years—and Barcelona, where our kids' grandparents lived, we'd choose to climb the mighty range separating France from Spain. We liked to approach the mountains any time of the year. In late October, the seasonal advance transforms the way light penetrates tree corridors or nearby mountain faces as deciduous trees change their color and, through chromatic oxidation, allow more light to get in.

Solitary mountain valleys such as the ones amid the peaks around Val d'Aran, in Catalonia, are never too distant from once-thriving rural communities that learned to cope with long winters, carrying animals from the valleys to the high mountain meadows in the summer months and back to the valleys when winter came. And, though transhumance was losing ground, some idealists were trying to start afresh in derelict hamlets clinging to boulders.

This is how we stumbled upon Emmanuel. A design consultant who converted to natural construction, Emmanuel Pauwels grew up in the Flemish flats of Belgium but decided to reinvent himself late in life. He found his new beginning in the mountains of Southern Europe. "I'm a late bloomer," he joked.

Pauwels's desire to search for "personal elevation" had nothing to do with religious views, early retirement, or social withdrawal. Quite the contrary: After purchasing a cheap ruin in a hilltop hamlet in the Catalan Pyrenees, he wanted to build a home that belonged to its place, keeping the name locals had used, Cal Guerxo. The restoration conceals an ambitious regenerative system that has attracted visitors worldwide. The home's location is also a privileged balcony upon a cliff overlooking a canyon, ideal for watching large birds of prey dancing with the winds.

He casually explained that the elements provide everything the house needs: orientation to the sun, rain collection, cross ventilation, and surrounding vegetation to feed the garden and offer the ideal temperature all year round—quite an accomplishment in a hamlet that easily stays below freezing on cold winter days. Emmanuel's eloquence kept our children tuned to the story, and even more so after they had some delicious homemade cake. Then, we walked through some of the home's enchanting secrets. As if by magic, or so our kids thought, a concealed antechamber captured the sun's heat and distributed it throughout the big home. Just when it was getting dark and chilly, we benefited from the slow release of stored warmth.

But that wasn't all: Using gutters and a first-flush system to clean the rooftop water, the home captures, consumes, and returns all rainwater to the garden annually. Nothing was going to waste, not even our own waste material: The gravity-flow composting toilets (on all floors) use a source separation system to ensure the urine remains sterile and is diverted to the garden.

After explaining how the natural pool has created a little ecosystem around its permanently flowing water, Emmanuel concluded, "It's not about being less bad, it's about being good."

We left wondering whether humans had forgotten that we had all built natural homes once. Could homes built in harmony with their context improve their surroundings?

Other restorations have more humble beginnings and means. In the Italian Alps, we were yet again awed by a photogenic, solo restoration project. Just a fifteen-minute walk from Johannes Schwarz's *rustico*, we met another new homesteader, then little known to the world, trying to plan his first winter in the area. (However, months after our visit, our video interview helped him become an internet sensation: After we posted our visit, the videos on his channel went from views in the low thousands to amassing tens and even hundreds of thousands.)

A reserved, slender man in warm clothes came to greet us. Martijn Doolaard introduced himself as a Dutch photographer who had documented his years-long bicycle travels around the world, but had decided to settle down and buy an old abandoned farm.

We followed him to two dry stone buildings in need of serious repair. Doolaard, a writer, expressed his comfort with the new property despite the Spartan setup; he had decided to embark on a quixotic "dirt cheap" renovation, he told us. The structures were in good shape, though pierced with holes between the stones. Doolaard had made camp inside one, using his tent and technical sleeping bag from his #bikelife days to begin renovating. A small solar setup allowed him to power electronics, lighting, phone and computer hotspot, and power tools. A wood-burning stove for heat and a bottle of propane for cooking completed the spare arrangements.

As we left behind the rough beauty of the peaks of Val Pellice, we engaged in a conversation about solitary life up in the mountains. The priest Johannes and Martijn, the globetrotting biker, seemed to share some common traits, such as the ability to thrive in solitude. Some people seem to flourish in places where others cannot.

ABOVE
When we visited, Martijn Doolaard had just started the renovation. Our video drove attention to Martijn's YouTube series, where he chronicles his homesteading endeavors.

OPPOSITE ABOVE
Before revamping a dirt-cheap abandoned stone farmstead in the Italian Alps, Martijn had been cycling around the world.

OPPOSITE BELOW
Can you live alone in the Alps and have more friends than ever? People tune in regularly to watch Martijn Doolaard's renovation.

OVERLEAF
Originally built as shelters for farmers and their animals, these two cabins are dry stone buildings.

OPPOSITE ABOVE LEFT
Black Kettle calls himself a "mountain man." He built his shelter "from scraps" on a friend's property in Idaho's high desert.

OPPOSITE ABOVE RIGHT
Leading a life rich in adventure, exploring "mountain living" for work and wanderlust.

OPPOSITE BELOW
Black Kettle has found his place by a pristine creek amid the sagebrush and lava fields. It's the rough, open landscape of Idaho's high desert flats.

ABOVE
He hasn't lived in a conventional home since 1974. His outdoor solar shower has inspired neighbors.

Crossing high peaks is not a small task. Today, the legendary Alpine passes are only used by skilled mountaineers or their contemporary extreme sports adherents. We imagined the task of crossing the mountains of the American West wasn't easy for the pioneers either.

Across the West's high desert, where sagebrush and giant stretches of volcanic bedrock complicate homesteading or even animal grazing, we have met some of the last so-called "mountain people." When we were introduced to Black Kettle in Idaho, an old and bearded solitary hobo with expressive eyes, he explained that the informal shelter in front of us was his first permanent dwelling since 1974, a place from where he was trying to start afresh despite the odds.

His house had come to life from scrap parts of other buildings, with collected windows and pieces from remodeling jobs. Old fence posts had become exterior walls and an outdoor bed. Outside, Black Kettle was growing a backyard garden with corn and amaranth. "Mountain living ain't that bad at this moment."

Like the people in this chapter, perhaps we all might one day enjoy a deeper relationship with the ways of the mountains and reconnect somehow with our adventurous, rustic selves. The mountains had cast their spell upon us, that was certain. We wondered if one day, not too far away, adventurous spirits will seek to establish bases in the peaks of other planets, from where they'd perhaps have the vantage point of enjoying the view of a small blue marble floating far away in space.

6. RESTORATION

After traveling across the known world, fourteenth-century Moroccan scholar Ibn Battuta, aka the other Marco Polo, realized that "traveling leaves you speechless, then turns you into a storyteller." He was onto something: Road trips can make us tired and cranky, yet they've been a blessing to us. Road trips with surprises along the way give meaning to a landscape, making it memorable and singular. Those are moments we remember, emerging from our consciousness by association with other events or sensations—like Marcel Proust and his famous madeleine moment.

No wonder our young family comes away from every trip with a renewed family bond. Traveling opens universes that only seem to manifest themselves while in motion. Learning from Marco Polo or Ibn Battuta, we make appointments along the road for pleasant discoveries while maintaining a structure and sense of purpose.

The design is a treat to the senses: With a curvilinear wood roof and two curved walls of windows, the home is enveloped in trees.

There have been many times we've been very close to missing the opportunity to meet legendary people. Consider the story of our encounter with Charles Bello, an architect-maker who settled long ago amid the redwoods of Northern California. Charles and Vanna Rae, his wife, had bought 240 acres of redwood forest in 1968, and, with little money and lots of work, they erected different homes, set up gardens, and connected DIY off-grid systems to support the family. More importantly, they managed to build with beauty in mind and on a budget.

Charles had started on the property as a recently married young man, going from the plan of setting up a tree farm to support his family to a lifelong quest to preserve his property's second-growth redwood forest for future generations to enjoy. He also designed and built the celebrated Parabolic Glass House, a modern organic home that expands like an accordion fan atop the property.

The house's transparent facade cuts the tree line in the far hills with an awning that functions as a sun cover, a testimony to his years as a young apprentice of innovative architect Richard Neutra. The design is a treat to the senses: With a curvilinear wood roof and two curved walls of windows, the home is enveloped in trees in the back, and it overlooks a sunken garden surrounded by an arch of solar panels right below the deck and a gentle meadow in downslope.

Yet we had almost missed Charles's story. Many years ago, Kirsten had received one among many emails. A call followed: A charming old fellow—energetic and talkative, West Coast old-school—explained that he had been living off-grid for fifty years up in the second-growth redwoods of unincorporated Mendocino. But intense fires prevented us from getting there despite our interlocutor's efforts. We tried to arrange a date to visit the year after, and we almost missed it again; that same week, we got a couple of unexpected appointments in the city. In retrospect, we are glad we did not call it off again. After driving for a long time on a dirt road, we finally found the gate to his redwood homestead.

PREVIOUS SPREAD
The house is set in a gentler dimension. To get there, one has to venture a half-hour down a dirt road leading to a redwood forest on the property.

OPPOSITE
Charles Bello learned architecture from Richard Neutra but developed his own compass, as shown in his Parabolic Glass House and attached garden.

OPPOSITE ABOVE
Charles built a circular gallery to display his sculptures, made mainly of fallen redwood trees. After seeing Kirsten's video interview with him, one commenter noted that Charles "deserves another lifetime."

OPPOSITE BELOW
The way river stones are chosen for a wall can offer the patterned visual equivalent of a musical melody: variation and repetition create beauty.

ABOVE
When Charles and his wife, Vanna Rae, arrived on their property for the first time, the area was fully logged, and the landscape was bare. Now, Charles likes to sit by the creek and see the water flow.

We were greeted by an enthusiastic character with contagious energy from the get-go. As he showed us his off-grid organic home, several outbuildings, and other charms of his vast property, we realized we were facing a special, unique polymath capable of gardening, building, making beautiful furniture, and turning wood stumps into sculptures.

Every second of our stay with Charles was worth it and unexpectedly refreshing. On our trip back home, we barely talked, but we could feel that our understanding of nature's patterns and the beauty of its variation through repetition was more profound after just *one* day with somebody special.

To Charles Bello, nature suggests potential designs that "guide" us to accomplish designs with a purpose. At one moment of our interview, Charles explained how he had come up with the fractal design of a glass facade where the wooden frame resembles the nerves of a leaf. After detailing the essentials of this design, he dismissed the title of "designer": "I don't design; I follow logic." At another moment, he showed how he had placed the different river stones on a wall inside his Parabolic Glass House, "like a melody," singing notes as he touched the stones conforming to the imaginary scale. In awe, we felt emotional a few times.

O ur serendipitous encounter with Charles Bello brought back memories from one of our first family trips, back when our oldest daughter, Inés, was a baby. In the winter of 2007–2008, we flew to Australia to attend a wedding in Sydney, then we traveled to Tasmania and Melbourne, discovering cities, mountains, and stretches of the outback by train, car, and on foot.

Once in Melbourne, we took the bus to get to the CERES environmental community to interview Bill Mollison, coauthor of the seminal book *Permaculture One* and the scientist and author who had taken the leading role in developing the concept of permanent agriculture, or permaculture.

When we arrived, we found a group of (mainly barefoot) youngsters was clustering around an older, neatly dressed figure with a trim white beard. He joined us minutes after. We will never forget the conversation that followed, which we videotaped.

ABOVE
Bill Mollison founded the Permaculture Institute in Tasmania in 1978. Thirty years later, in early 2008, we met him at an ecology center established atop a former garbage dump in Melbourne.

OPPOSITE ABOVE
Nico took this picture during our visit and interview with Bill Mollison, which we posted later on the web. Years later, somebody added it to Mollison's Wikipedia entry.

OPPOSITE BELOW
Bill Mollison talks about natural ecosystems to a group of students in Melbourne, Australia (January 2008).

We realized that "planting rain" wasn't a hollow metaphor.

OPPOSITE ABOVE
When Brad Lancaster and his brother bought their home in downtown Tucson, the streetscape was a dusty place devoid of trees or any vegetation. Things have changed dramatically since.

OPPOSITE CENTER
Brad's water-harvesting techniques borrow ideas from traditional stewardship and common sense to turn storm runoff into water that can be gathered to create an edible neighborhood.

OPPOSITE BELOW
Brad transformed an old garage into his "garottage" (garage + cottage) or "shondo" (shed + condo). His outdoor shower from collector water feeds the plants after use.

ABOVE
About 100,000 gallons (approximately 380,000 liters) of rainwater a year is captured on their property and surrounding public right-of-way.

We soon realized that Bill's concept of permaculture had germinated beyond Australia. One day we were having dinner on the terrace of our then apartment in Barcelona when we received a message from Tucson, the desert city in Arizona. Its subject read: "Idea: Planting Free On-Site Waters to Grow Regenerative Abundance." Brad, the message-writer, explained: "If you come back to the Southwest US, I'd love to show you the drought-proofing, flood-abating, resource-generating practice of 'planting the rain' or 'water harvesting.'"

Planting rain? Water harvesting? It certainly didn't sound conventional.

When we visited, we realized that "planting rain" wasn't a hollow metaphor. With patience and some community volunteers, Brad Lancaster had devised a way to use storm runoff and flash floods to nurture a complex ecosystem of native plants, whether growing on sidewalks or in backyards. Despite the area getting just 11 inches (28 cm) of rainwater per year, Brad's plan was proving that was more than enough water to revive a complex drylands habitat.

Before the change, in 1996, Tucson's dusty and desolate streetscape felt like an oven for most of the year. Now, through the planting efforts of Brad and his neighbors, the city hosts 1,400 mature native trees (some of which provide food) living exclusively on stormwater and thus preventing environmental damage. In fact, in 2004, after overturning early skepticism, the group was permitted to cut sections of the sidewalk to divert flood water from the streets into the tree basins.

Closer to home, Brad had more to show us, too. With a convivial and authentic enthusiasm, he invited us into the 200-square-foot (18 sq m)

garage he had converted with salvaged wood, relying on passive solar to heat and cool the place. (It was topped with a single small evaporative cooler for particularly hot days.)

On the eighth-of-an-acre garden he shares with his brother's family, Brad captures 100,000 gallons (approximately 380,000 liters) of rainwater per year and continues to experiment with greywater harvesting systems, fed with any water used around the house: sink, outdoor shower, bathtub, and washing machine.

Not long after visiting Brad Lancaster, we stopped by another landmark for environmentalism, restorative agriculture, and agroforestry: Aldo Leopold's farm. Leopold—the father of modern wildlife management, land regeneration, and wilderness conservation—died in 1948, but we sensed his legacy across the property. Here, his early experimentation with ecological restoration had encouraged him to try transforming abandoned farms—testimonies to overexploitation, dust storms, and the rural exodus of the Great Depression—into natural wonders.

In 1935, Aldo Leopold bought a worn-out farm along the Wisconsin River. With the help of his wife and five kids, he converted a former chicken coop into their weekend cabin, a place they dubbed The Shack. They immediately attempted to bring life back to Dust Bowl–era terrain.

ABOVE
Inside Brad's home. He uses passive solar to heat and cool the home, adding a swamp cooler on hotter desert evenings.

OPPOSITE ABOVE
"To plant a pine, for example, one need be neither god nor poet; one need only own a good shovel," wrote Aldo Leopold, perhaps peeking outside from this very window.

OPPOSITE BELOW
Leopold wrote his now classic book, *A Sand County Almanac*, on the property, which his family transformed from Dust Bowl barren land into a biodiverse forested area.

ABOVE
In 1935, Aldo Leopold bought a worn-out farm along the Wisconsin River. He took up residence in a former chicken coop, wanting his family to experience a life closer to nature.

Over the course of more than a decade, the family of seven planted fifty thousand trees, turning the degraded area into a lush landscape of conifers, hardwoods, and prairie. Leopold wanted to experience a life closer to nature. "Wilderness is the one kind of playground which mankind cannot build to order," he wrote in his now classic book, *A Sand County Almanac*.

We walked through the forest they had planted to get to The Shack. The old chicken coop appeared after a turn of the dirt road, a humble and vernacular wooden cabin. Inside, the wood was whitewashed.

The rather Spartan interior had just the essentials of life for a family visiting every weekend, and all the utensils were still in place. We imagined Aldo and his family going about their days, cooking in the small kitchen and relying on water from the well outside—and, on winter weekend nights, gathered around the living area's fireplace.

One of our kids asked where the family we had been talking about was. We explained that Aldo Leopold and his wife, Estella Bergere Leopold, had died a long time ago. And their children? They could be alive, though they'd be old, we said. Did we know at least their names? We looked for them: Starker, Luna, Nina, Carl, and Estella. Estella E. Leopold, the youngest of the siblings, passed away at age ninety-seven on February 25, 2024.

RIGHT
Nothing has changed inside The Shack, where Leopold, his wife, and their five children stayed while planting between three thousand and five thousand trees per year.

With an interest in blending a healthy diet with gardening, some communities are turning nonproductive land or even former concrete islands into "food forests," a series of trees, shrubs, bushes, vines, and vegetable crops that, combined, provide local benefits beyond their direct utility as food and interchangeable goods.

Ole and Maitri Ersson are a Portland-based couple in their early seventies who somehow look younger. In 2007, they decided to build the life and community they had been dreaming of. For the transformation to happen, there was just one little-big contingency: They were tight on money, so they used credit to finance the purchase of a rundown apartment building with a typical concrete annex of parking space.

With their own work and that of their tenants, they transformed the complex into an apartment-based intentional community. Now Kailash Ecovillage is a permaculture co-living space "with fifty-five happy tenants."

At the community's epicenter is a massive garden, made from the former concrete parking lot and now home to a food forest and co-living "agritopia." Kailash suits the community's emotional and practical needs, keeps them fed with healthy food, provides an opportunity for personal bonding, and has reshaped an underserved place into an aspirational one. Rents are kept low on purpose, and the Ecovillage currently has a waiting list of more than 300 people interested in moving in.

When we visited, the old apartment building had already been transformed into the current well-maintained property (with a new roof covered by solar panels) overlooking a lush garden. Walking through the garden with Ole, a couple of residents mentioned how the Covid pandemic had made them clearly see the importance of self-reliance in a moment of supply chain disruption, bureaucratic dysfunction, and social panic.

The residents at Kailash were eager to share their workarounds to secure food and water: They top their rainwater collection with strategic storage, and the garden and food forest yield year-round produce, while the building's sewage follows a process of natural pathogen sterilization before fertilizing the garden. It turns out "humanure" makes for great nitrogen and compost gardening supplements.

Would they want to improve anything? we asked. "Well, there's a long waiting list." Which meant that there were way more people interested in living in Kailash than places available. It was up to other communities to create such places. It was possible. "That's the message. It's possible," concluded Ole.

OPPOSITE ABOVE
Ole and Maitri Ersson bought a run-down apartment complex in the city and began to de-pave parking lots to make room for a community garden.

OPPOSITE BELOW
Where some see "work," most Kailash residents see joy and meaning; "it's an antidepressant; it's a way of creating food; it's a way of creating community."

ABOVE
Kailash Ecovillage is an experiment in urban regeneration, turning a bare apartment property into a thriving permaculture co-living space.

OPPOSITE ABOVE
When asked what is left to improve, Ole recognizes that there's a long waiting list to join the community, which is "accessible to all income levels."

OPPOSITE BELOW
Residents at Kailash help grow their own food, and their excellent, high-quality produce is sold at local farmers' markets.

Kailash isn't the only intentional community around using restorative techniques in depleted land near a city. Four years after our visit to Aldo Leopold's estate and foundation, we contacted another intentional community and educational center pioneering restoration agriculture. In 1994, we learned, seven friends had taken over a debt-ridden and derelict seventies-era organic farm north of San Francisco (the first organic agriculture easement in the country).

They had many doubts, but they shared a vision, and they set up shop to explore compatible ways of farming, wildlife restoration, and water management. Could they raise their families while restoring the land they would live in—*and* learning by doing during the process? They felt it had to be possible.

After three decades of operation, the Sowing Circle community near the Northern California town of Occidental is now a medium-scale alternative to suburban developments. Instead of homes detached from their surroundings and uninterested in improving areas beyond manicured rows of trees and individual lawns, their place shows it's possible to bring equilibrium to ecosystems while maintaining beauty and keeping edible gardens.

The area surrounding the Sowing Circle community, stressed in the last decades by resource depletion and the growing danger of droughts and fires, also benefits from the existence of eighty acres of restored land. But Brock Dolman, our guide, doesn't think there's such a thing as a template for sustainable farmsteading to be replicated anywhere. Instead, Dolman insists that people should listen to their predecessors rather than trying to follow strict formulas.

For example, in the Americas, modern agroforestry and multiple cropping can still learn from techniques once used along the Mississippi and in Mesoamerica before the arrival of Europeans, ones that are compatible with high-yield techniques with increased resistance to pests.

ABOVE LEFT
Wildlife and permaculture expert Brock Dolman is one of the original founding members of the Sowing Circle, an eighty-acre intentional community north of San Francisco.

OPPOSITE ABOVE
The Sowing Circle built five passive-solar small cabins they called "Solar Suburbia."

OPPOSITE BELOW
The property reuses its water, turns all waste into compost, grows its own food, and maintains a recognized plant nursery that includes rare and endangered food crops.

LEFT
In the early nineties, when
Mark and Jen Shepard
bought their property in
Wisconsin, it was a depleted
corn farm. They set out to
transform it.

nformed, self-reliant, real-life environmentalism did not disappear in Wisconsin with the Leopolds (page 122). In the early nineties, Mark and Jen Shepard left their life in Alaska and bought a cheap, degraded, 106-acre corn farm in Viola, Wisconsin. They began the ecological restoration of their property, transforming it into what they called the New Forest Farm.

Over three decades, Mark planted 250,000 trees, exploring natural patterns in a property that has become a valuable riparian habitat. A walk through the property shows the apparently aleatory patterns of the main agroforestry crops present: chestnuts, hazelnuts, and apples, followed by walnut, hickory, cherry, and pine (for the nuts). Several gardens hold annual crops, from grains to asparagus, and the roaming farm animals (cattle, pigs, lambs, turkeys, and chickens) provide valuable pest control and nutrients for the soil.

Mark's formerly depleted mono-crop farm is now a restored property that generates income: From seeds to tree breeds, Mark uses a method he's dubbed STUN: Sheer Total Utter Neglect. STUN involves planting trees at random with the greatest possible phenotype diversity and letting pests and diseases help him pick the best specimens.

Mark Shepard believes it's possible to replicate his "homestead paradise" everywhere. It will take time and there's effort involved, but nothing compared to the old days.

ABOVE LEFT
The Shepards transformed their 106-acre property into a perennial farm that has inspired people from around the world.

ABOVE RIGHT
Mark Shepard has developed a technique to breed the best-adapted trees, which he jokingly calls STUN: Sheer Total Utter Neglect.

7. UNDERGROUND

We've never lived in an underground home, but our experiences in them run deep. It's a long fascination we may have shared with other hominins: Like in the remote past, a cave protects us from the elements. During millennia, cave homes have hosted entire towns in Anatolia, Italy, Southern Spain, and France, to name a few. Such humble homes, a type of vernacular that vanished as living conditions improved and modern building standards developed, are now enjoying a revival as hobbyists and local authorities realize their historical value. They're also models of low environmental impact and adaptation to extreme conditions.

Unable to flourish while carrying on a conventional life, some people seem poised to seek adventures far away from their birthplaces, inspired nonetheless by the world they left behind. In the early twentieth century, citrus grower Baldassare Forestiere, a Sicilian immigrant with little education or training, arrived in the California Central Valley town of Fresno after purchasing some land sight unseen, with the intention of growing trees and farming. The hardpan soil he found upon arrival, on a desolate lot exposed to dry winds and punishing summers, changed all that.

With no money to start over and an unpromising property, Forestiere took a day job digging irrigation ditches, though he had a plan for his spare time: Affected by the California heat wave of 1906, the Italian immigrant dreamed a world of underground cool chambers much in the fashion of the old Roman vaulted chambers he had seen in his childhood. So, with just a pickax, a shovel, and a mule, he began excavating his future underground home and gardens, which today still stand outside Fresno, in California's agrarian San Joaquin Valley.

He spent decades excavating a fantastic world of rooms, tunnels, a chapel, an underground aquarium, and courtyards, where he planted

PREVIOUS SPREAD
Sicilian immigrant Baldassare Forestiere is famous for the the subterranean world he created, which took him 40 years (1906 to 1946) to build.

ABOVE
A feeling like no other: going underground in hot Fresno and finding the fantasy world built by Baldassare Forestiere.

OPPOSITE ABOVE
Tunnels and chambers lead to sunken courtyards where Forestiere planted many varieties of citrus trees.

OPPOSITE BELOW
Forestiere had no direct experience building but had seen arched structures growing up in Sicily and mimicked this ancient building technique.

ABOVE
Inside the labyrinthine underground realm created by this inspiring Sicilian immigrant, the perspective created by impossible openings, corridors, and steps reminded us of a real-life Escher painting.

citrus trees capable of bearing several different kinds of fruits at once. Twenty years after his arrival, he quit his day job to focus on selling his fruit and growing his underground world, reinforced with the ancient Roman technique of support arches, which he secured with self-made concrete and bricks.

When we finally made the trip to Fresno, we knew little about the man who had made this dwelling. The temperature cooled down as we drove further from the city, and the traffic noise from the nearby road vanished when we entered the first tunnel. We were immediately blown away by what Forestiere had accomplished: The labyrinthine home and gardens are a one-of-a-kind experience.

Walking across Baldassare's underworld paradise, we discovered verdant orchards 20 feet (6 m) below the surface, as well as his underground home and courtyard. Down in this magic realm, given the stable temperature year round despite Fresno's scorching summers and frost-free winters, all he needed for comfort were a kitchen with a wood-burning stove and an icebox, several cone-shaped openings for natural ventilation, and small summer and winter bedrooms.

Forestiere never married, though the underground complex he had created soon became a place for family gatherings and local conviviality; when he died in 1946, his brother Giuseppe and his children took on the duty of preserving the site. Today, the sixty-five surviving rooms include summer and winter bedrooms, a bath, a kitchen, a fishpond, and a parlor. These chambers are illuminated by the natural light piercing through the open-air courtyards, which in spring welcome visitors with the fragrance of citrus blossoms. Perhaps, the scent may have transported Baldassare to the childhood memories that inspired the artisanal archways, grottoes and courtyards he built by hand.

The house lay perfectly integrated into the hill as if it had spontaneously sprouted under it.

Somehow, Al Schwarz is a modern-day version of Baldassare Forestiere (page 136), pursuing his vision despite the odds. Decades ago, an IT job brought him to the Dallas–Fort Worth area. He used the move to pursue an unconventional project: Instead of settling for a suburban home near his office, he purchased an inexpensive farm lot near a small lake—seven acres for $49,000—and, undeterred by his lack of construction experience, began building a dome house into a small hill.

First, he boldly placed the prefabricated concrete domes that would form the main spaces of his home. Then, over the next ten years, he tirelessly moved 230 tons of rock and dirt, creating retaining walls and substrates for the grass and trees that now flourish atop his unique abode.

It was a rainy and windy day when we visited. The house lay perfectly integrated into the hill as if it had spontaneously sprouted under it, a sight that told us we were about to enter yet another "man cave" magical world, or, as Al said, "welcome to the coolest house around." Approaching the door, we could see through a spherical glass window that the entry was on an upper level just above the living area, with plants covering the railings of an elevated walkway.

Beneath the walkway, our host pointed out an indoor pond surrounded by water plants, and the kitchen, located just on the other side of the spherical window: We were "on the other side," like Alice in *Through the Looking-Glass*. The space had a movable counter designed

ABOVE LEFT
Al welcomed us to his enchanted seven-acre property near Dallas.

ABOVE
Al Schwartz wasn't going
to settle in a conventional
stucco box when he moved
to Texas from upstate New
York, so he built his own
man cave over the years.

by Al, and a glass table occupied the center of the spacious dome; further ahead, a big theater area with a projector formed his living room. (Al explained that neighbors would often visit on days when there were tornado warnings or extreme temperatures.) Other interconnected domes, also sheltered by the hill, provided space for the primary bedroom, guest bedroom, indoor garden, garage, parking, and plenty of storage space.

Before we left, Al presented us with "a little surprise" he had been preparing upon our arrival, though we needed to fly the drone to see it. What was it? When Nico put the drone up and flew it around the property, we could see that several species of flowers and bushes were planted to draw two gigantic images: a massive peace symbol and a giant yin-yang symbol.

LEFT
Al surprised us when he encouraged us to fly the drone: He had planted a yin-yang symbol and was "growing" a peace sign with flowers and bushes as well.

BELOW AND OPPOSITE BELOW
Al dug his home into the hillside to get low energy bills and protection from the elements.

P opular culture has often exploited our fascination for such organic, protective shelters. They frequently host very particular families. Enter the Lishmans in rural Canada. Bill Lishman began a small wildlife conservation effort by teaching geese how to migrate back home (and leading them across Canada in an ultralight aircraft.)

In fact, his quixotic adventure became a blockbuster film in 1996, *Fly Away Home*. It didn't surprise us that such a legendary family had decided to build an underground home to withstand Ontario's harsh winters and hot summers.

When we visited the Lishmans' house in 2018, Bill Lishman had sadly passed away; we were greeted by his wife, Paula, who showed us the home they had designed and built. After spending "too many winters" in a poorly insulated A-frame cabin, they envisioned a protective underground home that would keep them in perfect temperature conditions all year, and they began the project by knocking the top off a hill on their property, dropping in several ferro-cement domes, then covering it all up again with dirt.

They cut Gaudí-esque skylights into every dome (like the Pantheon's oculus in Rome), so their house remains naturally well-lit even in wintertime, despite being below the frost line.

After a quick tour of the unbearably hot original A-frame cabin, Paula opened the door of the subterranean home, and we were hit by cool air. There was no AC; this was simply the earth-cooled air characteristic of living below the frost line. We passed through the antechamber into the kitchen, where Paula stepped on a button and up popped their custom, round, lazy-Susan-style pneumatic fridge. We were enthralled, and the idiosyncrasies continued into the living room, where a huge swing hung from the domed ceiling and yellow glass cast a hue on the space.

To Bill and Paula, going underground had meant rethinking every aspect of living: Rooms were replaced by fractal concavities (they had eight), and all the furniture was rounded. The goal (and now, Bill's legacy) was not to simply "shove a square box under a hill" but to make a home truly in step with its surroundings.

ABOVE LEFT
Entrance to Bill and Paula Lishman's underground home sitting 15 feet (5 m) below ground.

OPPOSITE
A series of strategic skylights illuminate the home, which keeps warm in winter and cool in summer due to thermal mass.

ABOVE RIGHT
We found this humble mural depicting the adventures of Bill Lishman leading geese to fly home as he flies over his underground home.

On the other side of the Atlantic, in France, some nature lovers seem to have reached a conclusion similar to that of the Lishmans (page 145) and decided to return underground. Cave houses go back centuries in France, and some regions—such as the Loire and the Dordogne valleys—are known for their well-preserved examples, which people call *maisons troglodyte*.

Reviving a troglodyte home can be challenging but also economical—and life-changing: Such projects take the new troglodyte dwellers off the beaten paths of financing and permitting. En route from a friend's wedding near Nantes, we visited Henri Grevellec, a retired teacher who had decided to renovate an ancient troglodyte compound of six former homes outside the windy town of Grézillé.

Especially knowledgeable about his region's history and environmental challenges, Henri explained life at his home with passion. Living by himself in such a big cluster of troglodyte homes, he had turned just one of the dwellings into his cozy abode. A modern but humble kitchen and bathroom, a modest bedroom, and a dining room covered all his needs. He confessed to having indulged in just one feature: He had added a skylight in his bedroom to improve air exchange and bring a bit of natural light to it.

ABOVE
Henri Grevellec purchased a cluster of traditional troglodyte homes outside a windy town, transforming one into his house and using the others for storage.

OPPOSITE ABOVE
The homes are part of an abandoned quarry.

OPPOSITE BELOW
Our host shared fruit from his orchard with us.

Nestled below the
surrounding fields, the
circular courtyard facing
this troglodyte is sheltered
from wind gusts.

ABOVE
The unique Loire Valley
property made our children
feel like they were in a
fantasyland.

After the French Revolution, the houses that survived as humble shelters around villages did so as a testimony of past lifestyles and ways of living, and as a vector for social, environmental, and economic reinvention. Many years later, we stumbled onto another troglodyte restoration project less than one and a half hours by car from Henri Grevellec's dwelling (page 146).

In Amboise, known for the royal chateau that hosts the little chapel where Leonardo da Vinci is thought to be buried, Alexis Lamoureux, a young local, wanted to achieve financial independence. So, when the town sold—at a symbolic price—the derelict cave home that had belonged to his great aunt, he enlisted his Dutch girlfriend, Lotte van Riel, to help restore the structure and a little annex to use as their residence, turning the annex into a rental for extra income.

Unable to get a loan, the young couple invested in the dwelling's structural issues, revamping the interior themselves in their little free time while still working. "We were lucky enough to have a project and focus on it, so all the money we had we just invested it in the place," explained Lamoureux.

OPPOSITE
Alexis and Lotte restored two cave homes, occupying one of them while renting the other to help with household costs.

ABOVE RIGHT
Alexis Lamoureux at the entrance to his cave home.

A drive to play with a challenging project and the promise of turning a hobby into an opportunity for extra income—or even a new professional life in which to align vernacular restoration with the freedom of self-employment—led other people to pursue a similar trajectory with troglodytes across France. Not far from La Magnanerie, a noted cluster of restored troglodyte homes around an old site of silk garment production, Sandrine Lafage and her partner found a derelict compound with much work to be done.

The property at Noyers-sur-Cher, whose surroundings had hosted thousands of American troops during World War I, comprised the Moulin de la Motte Baudoin, a historic windmill, as well as a cave and a barn annex. The couple invested their savings in transforming the different dwellings, interconnected through an ancient maze of tunnels, into a B and B.

OPPOSITE
The windmill, caves, and tunnels were part of a vineyard and flour mill, later hosting American troops during World War I.

ABOVE
When we posted the video story on Sandrine's cave-and-moulin restoration, somebody commented: "A house that makes you feel like you're living in a Rembrandt!"

Waking up and stumbling upon the promise of the world's beauty at dawn, when everything still seems possible. During the Great War, these Rembrandt-worthy fields surrounding the cave and windmill hosted the tents of American troops sent to fight in Europe.

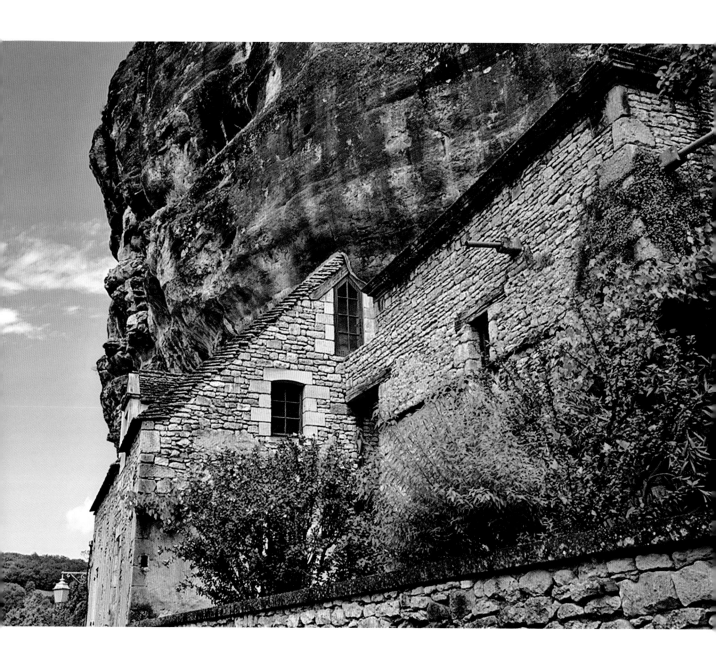

To those who haven't visited or seen any picture of it, the troglodytic village of La Roque-Gageac looks like it is out of an idealized world, with its picturesque homes built into gigantic boulders perching over a verdant valley and the Dordogne River below. Julien Cohen bought his first home, a small cave home ruin sprouting from the cliff in this Dordogne village five hours south of Val-de-Cher, as a fixer-upper bargain. He restored the derelict building on a budget, living in it as he improved it in his free time. Later, when it became too difficult for his growing family to live in, he turned it into a rental that provided the family with income.

Noticing the space that could open under a few massive slabs of rock, he created a megalithic home amid boulders.

I n the Americas, ancient native cultures and newcomers often built buried or underground dwellings in frontier territories. Today, some of us still dream of creating our own underground space, though few have gone as far as Steve Demarest. Amid the forested, steep valleys of Washington State's Cascade Mountains, in the Bavarian-themed mountain town of Leavenworth, this semiretired attorney transformed a rocky, unproductive lot across the road from his house by the river.

Noticing the space under a few massive slabs of rock, he created a megalithic home amid the boulders. Demarest now rents the space to skiers and excursionists, who are pleased to find it stays warm in wintertime and maintains its cool in the summertime due to the constant temperature of the dwelling's colossal thermal mass.

ABOVE
The rocks and steep terrain made Steve Demarest's property in the Cascade Mountains virtually worthless. To him, the area's cold winters and hot summers hinted at alternative ways of building to benefit from the Earth's thermal constant.

OPPOSITE BELOW
The entrance to his unique megalithic home is a secretive passage amid rocks resembling the entry of a Stone-Age abode.

OPPOSITE ABOVE
Demarest built a megalithic home after noticing how much his child liked to play there among the giant slabs of rock on the property. It took one month of drilling to get to a section where he could build a second chamber big enough to host a house beneath the solid boulders.

OPPOSITE ABOVE
The unspoiled rolling hills of Eastern Washington near the Idaho panhandle inspired do-it-yourself enthusiast Kristie Wolfe to build her dream underground home.

OPPOSITE BELOW
The abode's facade seems out of J. R. R. Tolkien: The facade blends post and beam construction with shingle-clad protection, whereas doors and windows are as round as those from Middle Earth.

ABOVE
Kristie Wolfe didn't want to spare any detail to inspire the cozy feel and sense of enchantment of a Bilbo Baggins-worthy home, including a carefully crafted round opening.

BELOW
Rather than relying on expensive furnishings, she got creative, repurposing abandoned and second-hand elements, from old mirror frames to turn into windows to the scraps of free wood that became the interior's unique cordwood floor.

N ot far from Steve Demarest (page 158), do-it-yourself enthusiast Kristie Wolfe bought a hilly rural property where she built an underground home "in the shire," inspired by survivalism in the American West and fantastic references from J.R.R. Tolkien.

Those who think fantasy books don't belong to reality should see Kristie's interpretation of the Middle Earth, this time in rural Washington state.

W olfe's folk-traditional approach to inspiring underground living contrasts with the modern, experimental take of one of the pioneers of underground building, both in the literal and in the conceptual sense. In 1968, like thousands of other back-to-the-land San Franciscans, Mike Oehler bought a property to build a homestead.

But, after a freezing winter in a small cabin, he decided to design the most affordable, best possible home to keep him warm in the wintertime and cool during summer. Oehler began his quest to explore underground homes, eventually writing the underground bestseller on the topic: *The $50 & Up Underground House Book.* Oehler passed away in 2016, not long after we visited him, writing to Kirsten a farewell email to keep fighting for useful content. Oehler had become the ultimate "Idaho modern old-timer" indeed.

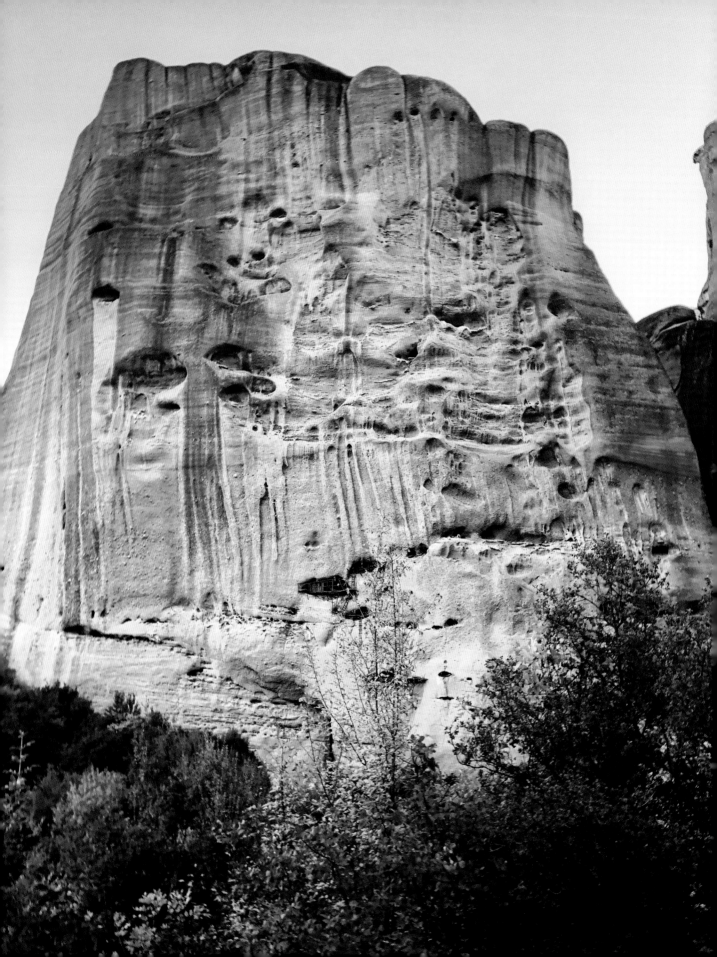

Greece also hosts a set of interesting cave dwellings, many are small cavities amid boulders and have been inhabited by hermits since ancient times. When we decided to take a ferry from Italy into Igoumenitsa, the passenger port in northwestern Greece not far from Ulysses's Ithaca, we made sure our endeavors through Epirus, Macedonia, and Thessaly left spare time in between to switch from highways to small roads and mountain paths, such as the ones leading to the carved-in humble hermit dwellings perched on the almost inaccessible boulders of Meteora.

Archeologist studies trace the origin of such secluded dwellings of wood, stone, and precarious masonry to the Paleolithic era, several millennia before Christians were attracted to the area's majestic landscape. The most primitive perched shacks pop out organically from natural caves and carved burrows on some of the most spectacular vertical boulders. With time, and with monasticism flourishing in Byzantine times, the early hermit dwellings were replaced by monasteries, which survived and even flourished under Ottoman rule. Lost in vertical dirt tracks among such Meteora remote boulders, we experienced the area's silence, isolation, and rough beauty, as if we were transported to the slow rhythms of geological time.

The future of such shelters seems brighter than some would think, though the reasons for the growing interest in underground dwellings are not always reassuring, as extreme weather conditions and the perceived risk of societal trouble rise in the century's third decade. At this point, we are too far apart from the twentieth century to keep blaming current issues on legacy mistakes.

Above all, Gaudí-esque, organic-looking sunken dwellings remind us of a remote past we can't quite picture but hold an intuition or two about, as if, in evoking life in a protective, cavernous burrow, we entered the oneiric world of a dream orchestrated by Salvador Dalí.

ABOVE
The first such shelters are nearly unreachable dwellings clinging to vertical boulders reminiscent of Yosemite's El Capitan.

OPPOSITE
From below, access to some of the areas where seclusion dwellings clustered is so steep that few from the villages below ventured there.

ABOVE
Many natural openings turned into shelters with added rustic enclosures made of vernacular materials.

LEFT
When we visited Meteora, we learned that the area had hosted hermits since time immemorial.

OPPOSITE ABOVE
Living amid cyclopes (the giants described by Homer in the Odyssey). A natural amphitheater of bare rock surrounds the village of Kalabaka in the municipality of Meteora.

OPPOSITE BELOW
It is not only an ancient Christian phenomenon: Archeologists argue that Meteora has been considered a holy place by hermits since the Paleolithic Age.

8. SURVIVAL

A ccording to Italian polymath Primo Levi, a survivor of Auschwitz, we all realize sooner or later that perfect happiness is unattainable. The good news is that the opposite feeling—perfect unhappiness—is equally unattainable, so there's that. Humans have made an art out of survival, and, like a chiaroscuro painting boldly carving light out of obscurity, some of the finest life-changing abodes come from seeking the light after their owners have had their deep dive into darkness. Did the progressive retraction of the geographical frontier shape the American character? One thing is clear: Depicted by Hollywood, the romanticized frontier has impacted the global collective unconscious. It has done so in different ways, though some fight the banality of everyday living by preparing for any disruption of the comforts we take for granted.

Endurance and survivalism influence many real-world projects we've visited, from doomsday homes to à la carte bunkers, as well as secretive disaster-proof getaways, extreme weatherproof dwellings, and makeshift minimal shelters for those who imitate Walt Whitman and want to "grow in the open air and eat and sleep with the earth." More than a reflection of real, imminent threats, some of these projects are an opportunity to experiment and test what we can achieve in a harsh environment, appealing to those who want to be proactive if things get rough.

Does the adventurous kid in us find fascination in survivalism? It would seem so, given the popularity of social media accounts that bring us closer to the lives of simple-living pioneers who decide to live a fulfilling existence under harsh conditions.

For example, the lives of our friends Jenna and David Jonas, a young couple growing a family with their dogs in a self-built log house amid the Alaskan wilderness, seem closer to an adventure book story than the average day-to-day. They are more on Thoreau's, or Jack London's, side, having spent most of their lives living off the land. At seventeen, David built a cabin in the woods of Vermont without power tools. He lived there for two years, learning to track animals, identify plants and birds, and navigate. When Jenna contacted us, they were expanding their own Arctic homestead on a remote lot they had found on Craigslist, living off the Alaskan wilderness, and already raising a baby with a big smile who, like a little Jack London character, is more accustomed to dog sledding than to city traffic.

Ten straight years of living in their boreal abode has changed their perceptions of time, patience, attitude, looks, and even the way they speak. With the Jonases, we entered a parallel world in which harshness and isolation have morphed into something wholesome and authentic in communion with their surroundings: Where some see mere subsistence, others see a connection with frontier life that we've lost. Jenna and David Jonas are a window to alternative lifestyles.

Above all, the young family reminded us that, when it's a choice, hunting, foraging, and growing most of one's food can be as fulfilling as our modern markers of status and success. Some move to bigger houses or buy a better car; others prefer to hand-build a smokehouse to cure the meat and fish and an underground root cellar to preserve their produce and potatoes throughout the year. Who is to decide what's better?

PREVIOUS SPREAD
Family life in an isolated cabin in the Alaskan Arctic requires a set of skills left fallow for generations: There's no supermarket to go to, whereas dog training, snowshoeing, ice fishing, wood carving, or gathering firewood and water are everyday activities.

LEFT
A traditional log cabin, built using only hand tools.

OPPOSITE ABOVE
Their adventures growing up in Vermont prepared Jenna and David Jonas to flourish in harsh environments.

OPPOSITE BELOW
When your backyard seems something out of a short story by Jack London.

There is winter, and then there's winter in the Alaska wilderness.

OPPOSITE ABOVE
Stacy and Guy Brand relish the unique off-grid experience of their modern home hideout.

OPPOSITE BELOW
Musubi House sits on a slope of Mauna Kea's volcano like a just-landed *Star Wars* rebel ship.

RIGHT
The house's diagram is geometrically simple: an outdoor triangle within an indoor triangle supporting a diamond-shaped roof. At golden hour, the off-grid hideout stands out like a gemstone.

Survivalism is a part of pop culture—and a growing one, becoming its own genre and promising heroic, personal salvation from extreme scenarios through a conscious, skillful effort. After visiting Jenna and David (page 170), we felt the need to expose our family (and audience) to the constraints of harsher times. Wired for survival, human cultures have dealt with disaster through stories teaching endurance, often inserted as parables within epic poems or religious rites. And, like our ancestors, survivalists seem wired for tales of preparedness and escape to doomsday hideouts.

When we flew into the Big Island of Hawaii in the late fall of 2023, we were ready to meet people prone to lifestyle experimentation, often despite false starts and setbacks. Among other acquaintances, we had been talking with Stacy and Guy Brand, the owners of a secluded modern house sitting on the green slopes of a forsaken giant volcano.

But we didn't know—that is, until we drove up the little winding road to its location—that the home, an off-grid hideout for an LA-based couple undergoing some serious health challenges, was going to sit on the landscape like a just-landed Star Wars rebel ship. The place made our children's imaginations fly.

Perched on a slope of the Mauna Kea volcano, arguably the tallest mountain in the world if measured from the bottom of the sea, and accessible only by four-wheel drive, Musubi House is powered by the sun and captures all its water from a huge trapezoid-sloped roof with a giant

rubber membrane. Yet everything works with the comfort of a high-end home built in some less exotic area.

Inside, the house immediately suggests the apocalypse-proof den that the likes of Mark Zuckerberg and Sam Altman wouldn't only approve of but envy. However, as guests staying at the owner's invitation, we were there to find its homey personality: We wanted to know whether a modern home like this one, with open-plan interiors and massive windows opening to the surroundings, could also have soul. "You are like being on a ship here… because you're dependent on yourself, the electricity, the water," is the way the contractor (and off-grid designer) Scott Dale explained it a few days later. "It's the same as a sailboat [but not] in the middle of the ocean."

During our stay, we found it hard to focus on everyday tasks. Our kids were postponing their homework as we cooked or planned shoots in our new, insular universe. At night, we looked at a sky with more stars than we had ever seen. Not even Nicky, our eleven-year-old son, could believably express his classic "meh, I've seen better" attitude. "It's crazy to think somebody may be looking at our planet from afar with his own problems and things to do," he said while looking at the stars. "Do you think these beings you are talking about are doing their homework as of now?" Kirsten replied. (Not a chance, Mum.)

And Nicky isn't alone in testing limits. As a civilization, we are well past our limit-testing safety levels. As in other eras of geopolitical instability and rapid environmental degradation, today's perceived significant threats feed an immune response in the collective unconscious.

ABOVE
Glass facades, skylights, and an open courtyard blur the lines between indoor and outdoor living, a very Hawaiian aspiration.

OPPOSITE ABOVE
The base of the home is a giant triangle with an inviting sunken living room in one of the angles.

OPPOSITE BELOW
Guy and Stacy Brand's shared working desk presides over the living room like a minimalist command center.

Dealing with uncertainty—that may be one of the reasons why we are attracted by the resourceful, MacGyver-like polymaths of the DIY world.

Retired Boeing inventor Paul Elkins is one of them, capable of turning old bicycle parts and the cheapest material available at a local hardware store into one-hundred-dollar mobile campers and makeshift, portable survival shelters. Based on Puget Sound's Camano Island north of Seattle, Elkins has designed inexpensive survival shelters with homeless and other underserved people in mind, imagining "wearable" gear that can deploy into essential nomadic dwellings, usually materializing as inexpensive micro-campers-on-wheels that can be pulled by a walking person or a bicycle.

We've visited Paul several times, and we're always amazed by the contrast between his nonchalant, can-do attitude and the bold micro-RVs, foldable boats, and camping gear he designs: They are a prepper's budget dream. His Lilliputian dwellings include little windows and places to cook, cost under $200, and can be pulled by bike. But they are more than a Burning Man toy, for they were also conceived to help alleviate homelessness.

ABOVE
These tiny campers can be easily pulled by bicycle.

OPPOSITE ABOVE
Paul Elkins has developed an array of tiny vehicles, folding boats, ultra-cheap shelters, and makeshift ideas to inspire others' DIY and survival endeavors.

OPPOSITE BELOW
This 9-sided deployable structure uses off-the-shelf foam board and 3-inch Gorilla tape to create a flexible, easy-to-transport survival shelter for under forty dollars.

ABOVE
Ron Hubbard has been building fallout shelters with complete amenities for more than a decade. He claims the factory he built is the largest bomb shelter facility in the world.

LEFT
A well-provisioned survival shelter.

ABOVE RIGHT
According to Hubbard, square-shaped shelters "feel more like a home" than the ones constructed inside giant metal pipes.

Current societal issues—real and perceived—feed a response of apparent resilience that could explain our fascination for entertainment around survivalism. But our collective idea of calamity and fear of the unknown has also turned fringe hobbies into a business. We have seen it firsthand, discovering makers specialized in creating and selling survival bunkers to anxiety-prone citizens. When we visited Ron Hubbard in the factory outside Dallas, Texas, where he makes metal-clad underground bunkers, he was on a phone call with Mira Ptacin, a *New York Times* reporter working on a similar story.

Hubbard's round structures made out of gigantic, corrugated culvert pipes would seem unreal—if it weren't the fact that he can barely keep up with demand. Hubbard, a Southern Californian now living in Texas, may be heading toward retirement age, but he isn't slowing down.

Once finished, his survival shelters (usually customized) include a toilet, shower, complete kitchen, dining table, bunk beds, and supplies for stays lasting weeks. Hubbard, a character as full of contradictions as the business he has created, explained to us that he keeps his clients list secret, though some of them are, according to him, notorious. They install such dwellings (which seem to belong to another era, such as the peak of the Cold War) under homes, sheds, swimming pools, or beneath empty fields.

To some extent, we seem to be living in the seventies all over again, although there's one stark difference: Nowadays, social media allows for easy commercialization (and banalization) of collective anxieties. Such is the case with survival shelters, some of which have been incorporated into boutique hotels or offered as short stay rentals. Escapism propels many of us to search for a "pristine" desert island or remote paradise.

Is it remote, though, if it's all over social media? Is there such a thing as sustainable travel? Is it possible to balance human impact and the economic benefits of visitors to local populations? Can our experience mapping the world be compatible with the rights of the last uncontacted human populations?

Some of our experiences as a family attest to the lack of actual remoteness in the era of TikTok. A few summers ago, we flew to Montreal, then drove several hours north to visit a tiny floating cabin in Lake Saint-Jean, Quebec's third-largest lake.

Little did we know that, to reach the floating cabin we had seen in an airplane magazine and then on the Web, our family would need to paddle there as darkness fell. When our car arrived at the lake shore, our host, Hugues Ouellet, quickly explained in French that there was no time to lose: We had a kayak trip ahead of us.

With a storm approaching, and just before it became too dark to navigate among the inlets, we spotted the blinking light of the cabin. (We knew we had a backup to contact if we needed help, but we were glad to have reached the place on our own.) That said, finding your way to a cabin in the middle of a remote Canadian lake would have been an experience too uncomfortable for most people just a few years ago.

Adventures like these are appealing, because they bring us off the beaten path and make us feel slightly vulnerable and uncomfortable (but not too much). What doesn't show in the magazine or on the Web is how exhausting they can also be.

ABOVE AND OPPOSITE
Lake Saint-Jean. After flying, then driving, then kayaking our way there, our family felt it had earned the right to enjoy the remote floating cabin.

OPPOSITE ABOVE
The loft is a greenhouse
floating cabin with a dock
for kayaks, a small kitchen,
and a composting toilet.

OPPOSITE BELOW
A sunroom of one's own:
The living room benefits
from sun exposure, which
warms up the cabin interior
despite Quebec's cold
climate.

ABOVE
When we arrived at the
lakeshore at sundown, we
had to hurry through our
kayaking lesson and safety
instructions.

f kayaking at twilight in Lake Saint-Jean may have felt slightly reckless, our visit to Andreas Ahlse's Spartan rural lodge of tiny turf dwellings in the Swedish forest feels like its European doppelgänger.

In Sweden, Ahlse, who had spent some time in the army, wanted to blend his career path in middle age with his predilection for forest survival with just a few essential tools, so he founded Kolarbyn—a collection of primitive huts made from mud, stone, and grass, each with just two slim beds and a fireplace, and a pioneering lesson in the field of bushcraft.

Ahlse built the huts just as the locals did for hundreds of years, when they were used as dwellings for workers who maintained the traditional charcoal industry. There's no running water nor electricity, just an outhouse and candles, yet Kolarbyn is as busy as it can be. "I think people are getting more and more interested in the old history and want to come out here and test how it was." In the era of all-you-can-watch streamed entertainment and of digital experiences that are getting more and more immersive, there's a growing interest in promises of back-to-basics experiences such as the one Ahlse provides in his remote hamlet: a bunch of tiny huts in a Swedish forest, where one can chop their own wood, start a fire, collect drinking water, bathe in the cold lake, visit the floating sauna, or pick some wild blueberries. Why this feels liberating is something we should ask ourselves.

In fact, it seems we can only reach conceptual and physical places we didn't know existed by embracing vulnerability—and a little discomfort. Philosopher and Holocaust survivor Hannah Arendt put it this way: "Man cannot be free if he does not know that he is subject to necessity, because his freedom is always won in the never wholly successful attempt to liberate himself from necessity."

Necessity stimulates adaptation processes involving generations, although sometimes it just takes one individual's curiosity and stubbornness to transform unconventional ideas into tangible places.

From reusable space rockets to extreme weatherproof dwellings to technologies that reach toward making life on the moon and Mars a reality, "naive" inventors (and pop culture) keep exploring the boundaries of the environments that will challenge our survival tolerance as a species,

LEFT
A forest like many others in rural Sweden conceals twelve well-camouflaged small cabins, all covered in mud and grass. They are part of Andreas Ahlse's back-to-basics primitive lodge: no electricity, no showers, and no convenience food or entertainment, just an unfiltered interaction with nature.

ABOVE
For hundreds of years, locals from the area surrounding Skinnskatteberg, Sweden, burnt charcoal for the iron industry and lived in rustic huts to stay close to the "coaling" process.

LEFT
To our children, the tiny huts in the woods were the stuff of dreams.

To preserve local tradition, the town of Skinnskatteberg built twelve charcoal huts from mud, grass, and stone. Inside, there's barely room for two single beds and a fireplace.

After a cozy night in a single bed warmed by a small fireplace in a charcoal hut, our kids stepped outside and picked fresh blueberries straight from the surrounding bushes to complement their breakfast. Years after, they still recall the experience.

9. RESURRECTION

When on the road in search of stories and adventure in a broader sense, we've both consciously sought and randomly stumbled upon ghost towns, and, like Tolstoy's famous opening sentence, we've realized that all inhabited villages are alike, but each ghost town is particular in its own way. In this chapter, we visit a trove of adventure seekers, rogue characters, and idealists who are trying to revive defunct towns—or create new ones from scratch.

Abandoned towns don't only belong to the world of relics and vestiges we call "ruins." They are remnants of activity—and, sometimes, prosperity—in the past, removed enough in time not to bother anyone, but close enough to reflect recent events and memories. On both sides of the Atlantic, such towns have often had invisible ties, times when entire hamlets in Europe emptied as their inhabitants left for nearby industrial areas or the Americas. Paradoxes of history, the frontier's boomtowns later became ghost towns, often leaving traces of their previous immigrant populations from the Old Country. How many ghost towns have our ancestors left behind?

We were greeted by permaculture gardens surrounding many structures, each one a whimsical self-build: a hobbit home, a treehouse, a tiny A-frame, a small roundhouse.

When Dan Schultz moved from Flint, Michigan, to the West Coast, he wasn't seeking ancient ruins to revive, he was just looking for a fresh start, far away from the Midwest. He had been told his dreams of building an ecovillage amid nature were foolish (or worse), but he wasn't looking for conformity or peer approval, so he bought 160 acres of forest land in remote Northern California. The raw, hilly land he bought between the enchanted world of Jedediah Smith Redwoods State Park and the Oregon border had plenty of second-growth lumber and gravity-fed water, and enough sunlight to gather solar energy and grow food.

When we first visited Schultz, it was early summer. We met him as he was making the uphill drive back from the hardware store with a vehicle full of supplies. All maintenance, he told us, cost him around $5,000 per year, including taxes, propane, and building materials for more cabins. We were aghast for the first time that day, though it wouldn't be the last; here with Dan, the rules of physics and civilization's constraints didn't seem to apply.

We followed him along a dirt road meandering through the mountains to reach his secluded property. Further along the drive was a small bridge over a creek, but Dan didn't bother to take it—we watched as his Tacoma, packed with building material, plowed across the water with no hesitation. Not long after, we spotted a long, window-clad building perched on a hill like a giant resting dragon: This was our first encounter with the Earthship Solarium, a massive DIY construction stretching nearly the length of a football field and providing year-round produce and potatoes, as well as shelter at its eastern end.

As we continued up the hill, we were greeted by permaculture gardens surrounding many structures, each one a whimsical self-build: a hobbit home, a treehouse, a tiny A-frame, a small roundhouse (Dan's private quarters), and a main lodge that Schultz and the eight other permanent community residents share. At the top of the property, Dan had transformed an existing round home into dorm-style lofts tucked into the natural setting.

PREVIOUS SPREAD
At Matt and Jenny Swarbrick's farm in North Wales (p. 196), we almost missed this turf-covered, half buried cabin overlooking the Irish Sea.

OPPOSITE ABOVE
The Solarium, a mountain-long Earthship where Dan Schultz grows food all year round, includes living quarters where he stayed while he was building it.

OPPOSITE BELOW
All the structures on the property were whimsical self-builds. When a fire spread through the area in 2023, several of them survived, including this hobbit dwelling.

OPPOSITE ABOVE
When we visited Dan's off-grid village near the California-Oregon border, several people lived in it and stayed at the rentals he offers. This structure served as a kitchen and socializing lodge.

OPPOSITE BELOW
After the fire, Dan was finishing a mosaic depicting the phoenix rising from the ashes on the rebuilt main building.

ABOVE
Dan had to evacuate when the Smith River Complex mega-fire hit the area. When he returned, he recorded a video of the loss.

Unfortunately, wildfires destroyed this idyll just a few months later. We shared Dan's call for help with our community at *faircompanies and they responded, but we were not optimistic when we visited again at the end of the same year, thinking we were about to enter a barren territory. We were wrong. We had clearly underestimated Dan Schultz—and nature's regenerative power. The drive was indeed sad; much of the forest was gone, though tree stumps and bushes were sprouting everywhere. But when we crossed the creek, we were relieved to see that the giant Earthship Solarium was intact. The dorm building and lodge were also gone, but a replacement on top of the surviving foundation was complete and with work underway to finish a mosaic inside near the chimney. As we came closer, we saw a skillful, colorful mosaic depiction of a phoenix rising from the ashes.

Today, the Earthship, the hobbit home, a greenhouse home, and Dan's roundhouse are occupied, and the garden is providing food once again. The NorCal ecovillage isn't going anywhere. Dan is thankful and full of projects for the future.

Matt and Jenny Swarbrick at their farm's gate in North Wales. When they found this abandoned quarry between the mountains and the Irish Sea, they liked that it had "a bit of everything."

A love for nature can take different shapes. We've met many people who think it's time to go from theory to hands-on approaches.

Welsh regenerative-agriculture enthusiast Matt Swarbrick is one of them. Matt once believed he had found his calling in exploring ecosystems worldwide with the crew of the BBC series *Planet Earth*, where he worked, and which would have been considered a dream job by anyone.

But, more than a decade ago, Matt—quite a jovial, high-spirited, genuinely funny man—decided to leave behind city life and TV production to, in his words, "grow cabbages and children." He settled on eighty evergreen acres of former quarry land at the northwest corner of Wales, between the mountains of Snowdonia and the Irish Sea.

Just a few miles south of Bangor, the oldest city in Wales, after driving through what must be the narrowest tarmac winding road we've ever driven, we saw firsthand why Matt had traded travel and adventure for a quest to "learn every bird's nest" in his own corner of the world. Dubbed Henbant Permaculture, the property had a bit of everything, from green pastures overlooking the Irish Sea to a forested area facing the Welsh peaks, so Matt, along with his, wife, Jenny, a geologist and water-flow expert, began using permaculture techniques and regenerative farming to restore the soil and prepare the vegetable beds. Today, the one-acre garden grows produce to feed one hundred families.

The couple planted to convert pastures into savannah grasslands; they also restored woodland edges and planted fruit and nut trees. They left small spaces for the rotational grazing of cows, sheep, and chickens, "with the exception of this one, which refuses to be a chicken," explained Matt, laughing as he pointed at a free-range chicken going about freely in front of him. That's how we met Strawberry, an anarchist-leaning, individualistic hen.

After restoring a small stone farmhouse already on the property, Matt and Jenny opened the farm to permaculture workshops and stays in nature, creating a campsite and roundhouse first and building vernacular cabins soon after. The traditional Celtic roundhouse, tucked away in a forest as if out of a Tolkien incantation, was proof, Matt joked, that we had entered the "fairy lands." Its red, round walls were made of cob, straw bale, and lime, and topped with a sod roof. Soon after, we left the forest and arrived at a meadow, fresh and as bright green as a Celtic dream.

When Matt started talking about another structure on the spot, we asked where it was. "Look carefully," Matt stated, smiling. Then we noticed a turf-covered, half-buried cabin in front of us, which they describe as "a mix of Viking longhouse and underground hobbit hideaway." It blended with the landscape of rolling hills, stone farmhouses, and sea so seamlessly that it wasn't difficult to feel carried away to another time and dreams of legends.

ABOVE
Matt Swarbrick enjoyed what many would consider a dream job, working for the BBC's *Planet Earth* series. Then he decided to kickstart his own regenerative farm in rural Wales.

OPPOSITE
To supplement their income, the Swarbricks launched workshops and built dwellings for guests to stay in, like this Celtic roundhouse in their "fairylands" forest.

M eanwhile, in another country much further south, the high-altitude meadows on the Pyrenees foothills have attracted shepherds and their roaming flocks every summer for generations (until modernity and the Spanish Civil War—especially cruel in disputed areas—all but ended the tradition).

Tens of such hamlets, scattered along the Pyrenees and the mountain slopes of the Ebro Valley, lost their populations during the conflict, and others emptied when their last inhabitants migrated to cities.

But now, two are being revived and transformed by intentional communities. Empty for decades, and partly reclaimed by the forest, the villages were fast becoming public land when a group of self-styled pioneers settled in and began restoring many of the abandoned structures. The hamlet in northern Navarre (not far from the forests along the Irati River described by Ernest Hemingway in *The Sun Also Rises*) has been transformed into an *ecoaldea* (ecovillage) named Lakabe.

It all started in the early eighties, when Lakabe's new inhabitants came from the city with little to no knowledge of country life. No one bet on their determination, but they stuck to their dream and managed to rebuild the homes and gardens despite the lack of a paved road, carrying the construction materials by horse, reusing things on site, and relying on candles and oil lamps until they were able to set up their first off-grid system.

Soon, paths and gardens sprouted between the main lodge—which hosts a communal kitchen—and several restored stone houses, stables, and even a windmill erected by hand. The community learned to live with little money, earning some income by working odd jobs in the area and selling organic sourdough bread from their bakery. Decades later, Lakabe is a self-reliant tiny society that generates its own food and energy thanks to the windmill, solar arrays, and a water turbine.

ABOVE
Lakabe residents were commuting from the city but soon learned masonry and sustainable agriculture techniques to create a self-reliant community with little need for money.

OPPOSITE ABOVE
Lakabe had been abandoned for decades, hidden within the overgrown forest, until a group of friends settled in and brought it back to life.

OPPOSITE BELOW
These restored Basque-vernacular houses aren't far from the forests along the Irati River, described by Ernest Hemingway in *The Sun Also Rises*.

"When we came here, it was to try to live closer to nature, closer to certain values that were disappearing from this urban world."

Days after visiting Lakabe, we met Ricardo, a resident of another restored medieval town less than an hour away but deep in the Aragonese Pyrenees. After being abandoned during the Spanish Civil War, the picturesque village of Ibort, a cluster of stone houses around a little church presiding over a meadow, had remained empty for decades. In 1986, a group of friends, all urban dwellers, decided to adopt a slower life in the country.

"When we came here, it was to try to live closer to nature, closer to certain values that were disappearing from this urban world," Ricardo explained. He and his neighbors learned masonry and gardening "by necessity." At times it wasn't easy, but they managed to restore many houses.

Now, the abandoned church has become a meeting place for the new inhabitants, and the village of Ibort lives by its initial goals: following the cycles of nature, building simple homes, and growing most of the food consumed year round.

Both Lakabe and Ibort have eluded their previous destiny of erasure, yet their inhabitants face new concerns, having been "discovered" by tourists seeking "authenticity." This risks opening the door to the construction of weekend homes in the picturesque rural area. Such has already been the destiny of several mountain hamlets, like the nearby valley of Aran, which was developed into a ski resort.

As Portuguese writer José Luís Peixoto once observed, "now, the rural is the revolutionary." For people like Peixoto, rurality shows more possibilities of personal emancipation and intellectual nurturing than bland urban—and suburban—life.

But now, some inhabited hamlets, such as a picturesque cluster of schist villages (Aldeias do Xisto), attract urbanites willing to exchange buzzing Lisbon for a slower pace.

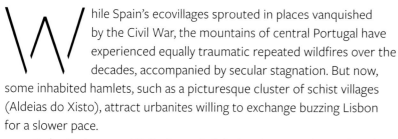

While Spain's ecovillages sprouted in places vanquished by the Civil War, the mountains of central Portugal have experienced equally traumatic repeated wildfires over the decades, accompanied by secular stagnation. But now, some inhabited hamlets, such as a picturesque cluster of schist villages (Aldeias do Xisto), attract urbanites willing to exchange buzzing Lisbon for a slower pace.

Pedro Pedrosa and Sofia Sampaio left the city more than a decade ago for Ferraria de São João, a schist village nearly obscured by eucalyptus trees that had taken over the area. Pedro set out to revive the rural ecosystem, first restoring several stone outbuildings that would become home, then transforming three stone storage sheds into modern homes built with local materials: cork, pine, lime, and slate.

To keep future fires away from the village, Pedro and other residents planted local cork oaks (which are more resistant to fire) around its perimeter. It worked.

ABOVE LEFT
The area had been ravaged by fires magnified by the excess of flammable eucalyptus trees, a local monocrop. Pedro Pedrosa came up with a plan to grow a ring of native cork trees that serve as protection against future fires.

ABOVE RIGHT AND OPPOSITE
Pedro Pedrosa and Sofia Sampaio have restored several small homes and stone outbuildings using local building materials such as cork, pine, lime, and slate.

The rural diaspora of Central Portugal has its counterparts in other areas. In the Alpine area of Piedmont bordering dreamy Lake Maggiore, Maurizio Cesprini and Paola Gardin created a laboratory of rural regeneration around the abandoned hamlet of Ghesio (Ghesc, in Piemontese). The village cannot be accessed by car, but this didn't prevent them from restoring one of the hamlet's stone houses. Despite having just three permanent inhabitants (the couple and their son, Emil), other houses are being rebuilt, pioneering a movement blending remote work with hyperlocal living.

LEFT
With €25,000 and one thousand hours of work, Maurizio Cesprini and Paola Gardin rebuilt a ruined home in the Alpine village of Ghesio.

ABOVE
Maurizio and Paola have turned their abandoned hamlet into a rural regeneration laboratory, hosting workshops to teach historical stone construction techniques.

Miller knew the town's buyer, who told her she could pick a ruin to rebuild.

nspired by a wealth of internet resources and remote work, DIY enthusiasts have turned to rural, often picturesque areas that suffered depopulation and dereliction. Armed with small budgets and a "learn by doing" attitude, their shared goal is to bring these old houses and hamlets back to life.

Some consider themselves "neo-rurals" or "back to the landers," while others talk about "geographical arbitrage," or living somewhere affordable while still earning a city salary. A case in point in West Texas is Terlingua, a dusty ghost town near the border that brings the visitor back to Western and postapocalyptic cinema classics.

Terlingua was once a mining boomtown supplying the United States with forty percent of its quicksilver needs for gunpowder in 1922. When the mine closed in the 1940s, the settlement of semi-temporary wooden houses and saloons, as well as dry stone constructions, emptied out and soon faced erasure.

The town had an opportunity at resurrection in the 1980s, when somebody purchased the site. But when we visited a few years back, only a few people bothered to visit the town's desolate graveyard, which seemed out of the movie set of a spaghetti Western. Now, the town blends experimental construction that seems to belong to the Burning Man venue, which is neither traditional nor futuristic, just in another dimension. A few RVs and modular structures pop up amid more permanent stone homes, such as Mimi Webb Miller's, a local who greeted Kirsten when we walked around town on a scorching hot day. Miller knew the town's buyer, who told her she could pick a ruin to rebuild: "There was just one room. It wasn't even a room; it was a doorway and a box sitting on some rocks. So, the rocks were left, and the adobe was all gone. I started building in '96 and very quickly had a home."

OPPOSITE ABOVE
Near the Rio Grande wastelands of West Texas, the ghost town of Terlingua, once a thriving mining town in the desert, came back to life as an alternative community after decades of neglect.

OPPOSITE BELOW
In July 2016, we visited Terlingua in a Prius with little more than a cooler and a tent to withstand the night in the desert. Our children played in the ruins, which looked like a passage out of Cormac McCarthy's Border Trilogy.

OPPOSITE ABOVE
Mani is the central of the
three peninsulas that dive
into the Mediterranean
southward from the
Peloponnese in Greece.
A place of austere stone
defense towers, it's the land
of the Maniots, who claim
descent from the ancient
Spartans.

OPPOSITE BELOW
Four decades ago, Kostas
Zouvelos, then a young
idealist visiting Mani, saw
that a crumbling fortified
tower was for sale, and he
and a friend bought it on
the spot.

ABOVE RIGHT
The property overlooking
the Aegean Sea is now a
three-room retreat, perfect
for reading Aesop or Homer
while daydreaming.

egarding ancient ghost towns and Spartan restorations: In ruin-rich and sparely populated Mani, the Grecian middle peninsula, south of the Peloponnese Region, derelict farmsteads and country houses can be legally rebuilt as long as the old site has a cadastral record—a register of property ownership. Almost four decades ago when vacationing there, Kostas Zouvelos and Kassiani Theodorakakou stumbled upon a derelict nineteenth-century fortified tower. It was for sale and very affordable, so they bought it before deciding what they would do with it.

They spent eight years converting their collapsing tower into a very particular three-room guest house using a traditional mortar technique called *kourasani*: lime, local soil, river sand, ceramic powder, and a small amount of cement. The 270 square feet (25 sq m) per floor required imagination, so the couple installed a kitchen and lobby on one floor and three bedrooms on the remaining stages, connected via a trap door as if from some sort of ancient vertical shotgun design. Kostas told us that taking care of the tower has been his life since.

Our travels visiting revived ghost towns and abandoned houses made us wonder what makes a good shelter and which modern tools, such as off-grid setups and reliable internet connection, allow people to live at a fraction of the costs they would face in conventional housing markets. This story of regeneration—and the integration of the "rural remote" in our cultural and physical proximity—has just begun.

10. FUTURE

Thomas Edison defined discontent as the first necessity of progress. However, once at home, most optimists seem to forget about innovation and stop dreaming big, living in spaces not much different than those used by their ancestors. And, even when they look traditional, today's houses can make people sick due to indoor air toxicity. If we like our homes the way they have always been, why introduce materials and layouts that make us sick?

Antoine de Saint-Exupéry, the French aviator-author, wrote that perfect designs are attained by removing what doesn't work: "In anything at all, perfection is finally attained not when there is no longer anything to add, but when there is no longer anything to take away, when a body has been stripped down to its nakedness." Why not follow the same approach when designing homes?

By detecting the things that don't work, we could be in a better position to build and restore homes that are beautiful, comfortable, and affordable. Making places bigger to hoard more things we don't need doesn't seem like a strategy that will bring bliss to a household.

f we were to draw a conclusion from all our collected videos, it would be that homes turn out to be "life-changing" when they prevail as places that balance beauty and utility and are patina-friendly. They gain a timeless character as they adapt to host the people inhabiting them, keeping them healthy (and safe). Some timeless construction techniques come from vernaculars that responded to previous environmental challenges, social tensions, and even individual or collective trauma: drought, pandemics, forced migration, or destitution.

For example, the devastation of wars and natural disasters prompts communities to appoint architects and designers to build easy-to-deploy homes for the unhoused. Today, the main stressors aren't open war and destruction but a lack of affordable housing, while climate threats make previously safe areas more expensive to insure. With a constant need to maintain and rebuild, why not use modular and prefabricated techniques developed during conflicts to design homes where people want to live— and can afford to do so? Kit homes are not a new idea: More than a hun-

PREVIOUS SPREAD
Can a house adapt to life in an environment as harsh and demanding as the high desert of New Mexico? The experimental Earthships of Taos aspire to emulate the resilience of native desert plants, immune to droughts, strong gusts, and dramatic temperature changes.

ABOVE
Living in small apartments and seeing very compact spaces, we also realized that it's not the layout, but the 3D space that matters, so the design is high enough for two-story configurations.

dred years ago, people migrating to places in Europe, Australia, or North America would acquire them by catalog through Sears—and assemble them on site. But the idea never quite lived up to expectations.

Over the years, as we visited people and heard their stories about their lives and the homes that contained more than meets the eye (a material world, but also one of hope), people kept asking us: If you were to build a simple home, what would it look like? So we decided to build a prototype with the help of a few friends, among them the architect and the carpenter who had assisted us in restoring our country home one hour outside Barcelona. We launched the idea in the spring of 2024, calling it Biokabin and starting with two goals: This ideal home had to be light on the land—high livability, low impact—and, secondly, we weren't interested in building a one-off model just for us, so it needed to be crafty but easily replicable.

But the real challenge was this: Could we build it ourselves without fancy tools? With that in mind, we designed and built a modular prototype that can be as small as 100 square feet (9 sq m) for a single module to as large as you'd like by simply adding modules, and tall enough to allow for two-story setups—an attic or mezzanine today, an open-plan tomorrow.

Biokabin's components are cut in a factory and can be assembled with just a few people using a wrench and a ladder (no need for a crane). To us, the future of housing can aspire to blend with the landscape, having a net positive impact on a given community. And a flat-pack design made of wood could evolve with its inhabitants: Thanks to its modular design of interchangeable panels, it can grow and shrink and can be moved from one place to another. By dreaming, we're trying to start a conversation that may inspire others in their search for their life-changing home, whatever that means for them.

We also have noticed that, despite the interest in "smart" and "efficient" homes, few people ask for healthy homes, despite living amid an epidemic of bad indoor air quality thanks to the pervasive use of volatile organic compounds (VOCs) in building materials, furnishings, and many things that have that characteristic "new car" smell.

According to scientific research, modern buildings interrupt our ancient symbiotic relationship with microorganisms from the environment that keep our overall health in check, helping propel allergies, autoimmune diseases, and cancer.

But many people realize that "healthy homes" are not just houses with greenery outside but are those using actual materials, finishes, and furnishings that don't off-gas, are plant or mineral-derived, allow for a certain grade of permeability, and make a building ultimately biodegradable. We've also been asked: Is it possible to build a home for the future that is healthy and biodegradable? It's not only possible, but we've talked to amateur builders and architecture studios whose goal is building natural homes that combine comfort and porosity, so they stay healthy—both to live in and to mess around in—particularly for people with autoimmune diseases, pregnant women, and babies.

OPPOSITE ABOVE
Historically, Washington, D.C., has used back alleys to build small infill neighborhoods, so Andrew and Hannah Linn decided to tap into this tradition and transform a parking lot into a natural home built with compostable materials.

OPPOSITE RIGHT
As an architect and a young father, Andrew Linn is pioneering healthy building techniques that avoid using materials that off-gas.

OPPOSITE ABOVE
Jack Becker calls this backyard home studio the Grass House. He designed it along with his architecture partner, Andrew Linn, as a natural materials manifesto to bring back beautiful, healthy dwellings in the D.C. area.

OPPOSITE BELOW
Simple and proportional, the Grass House's facade shows a vernacular, tranquil elegance, ready to withstand the passage of time gracefully.

ABOVE RIGHT
When you enter Jack's tranquil backyard home studio, it smells of drying grasses, in stark contrast to the off-gassing, more typical new home odors of paint and drywall.

n the D.C. area, young architects Jack Becker and Andrew Linn also build structures that are attentive to the vernacular style using healthy materials, usually sourced within their region radius. Their office is a natural materials masterclass, and Andrew Linn and his wife, Hannah, live with their baby in a cork-wrapped compostable home erected on an underused D.C. alley parking lot. They didn't pay more nor did they give up anything to accomplish their dream. Quite the opposite.

n California's Gold Country up in the Sierra Nevada, Neil Decker and Stella Michaels made their dream a reality by doing some of the work themselves, having attended building classes in the past.

They built a natural roundhouse whose main materials are hemp, lime, sand, wood framing, metal (for the roof), and nails. Dealing with autoimmune issues, they decided to explore the possibility of using hempcrete walls. Their hazardous chemical–free home is comfortable and insulated while permeable, and it has turned out to be the place where they can flourish.

ABOVE
Neil Decker explained that the round layout came naturally to them after observing the pattern repetition of spirals in nature, from galaxies to draining water, nautilus shells, and many other plants and animals. Why not use the spiral's mathematical efficiency in a house's interior?

OPPOSITE ABOVE
Neil and Stella had experience with rammed earth construction, and they built their roundhouse using hempcrete (hemp, lime, and sand). The outcome is a breathable home that adapts seasonally thanks to passive heating and cooling through tubes buried underground.

OPPOSITE BELOW
Neil and Stella now want to focus on the house's surroundings by reducing fire hazards and growing a garden.

n the picturesque Catalan region of La Garrotxa, near the Spanish Pyrenees, Nil Camarasa and Olivia Manzart sought an affordable way to build their dream natural home. So they combined a prefabricated system, with the foundation of a timber-framed home, with hempcrete and lime walls. Theirs is a modern-looking dwelling with all the comforts of a contemporary home minus its hazards, and they accomplished their project at a similar cost to conventional construction in their area.

ABOVE
With no building experience, Nil Camarasa and Olivia Manzart decided to self-build a natural home that didn't sacrifice the positive aspects of modern life.

BELOW
Inspired by La Garrotxa's culinary tradition, Nil and Olivia improvised a delicious dinner with a few fresh ingredients.

ABOVE
In 1960, futurist Buckminster Fuller imagined a geodesic dome over Manhattan to regulate microclimates better. The closest he got was Montreal's Biosphere, a twenty-story-high structure of self-reinforcing polyhedrons built as Expo 67's American pavilion.

A ll of the houses you have seen so far in this chapter are innovative in many ways; some of them are partially or totally biodegradable, and Biokabin tries to combine modularity with attention to place and people, traditionally more associated with vernacular construction. Yet, when we think about the future, what comes to mind are images of *Futurama* and flying cars, fifties-style, or perhaps the dystopian landscapes of *The Fifth Element* (New York City in the mid-twenty-third century) or *Blade Runner* (Los Angeles, decades ahead).

The car-centric society displayed in another Futurama, New York's 1939 World's Fair, advanced the vision of a society twenty years into the future that was dependent on superhighways. But does the future need to look like the imagined images that science fiction writers and filmmakers had of life after World War II? Undeterred by conventional shapes, materials, or layouts of homes or cities, futurists like Richard Buckminster Fuller envisioned a world of plenty after the Second World War.

Dreaming of mass production, Fuller combined the metallic fuselage of modern airplanes with designs from nature to come up with round shapes capable of self-reinforcing themselves with the minimum amount of material, like the geodesic dome. His dreams never materialized, and most people were against domes and their round layouts.

We grasped Fuller's ambitions when we visited Montreal's Biosphere, a spectacular twenty-story-high spherical structure of steel polyhedrons he built as the American pavilion for the city's Expo 67. The morning we approached the building after flying in from Paris, we wondered about the links connecting Fuller's biggest-built geodesic dome with Gustave Eiffel's tower. The latter had also been built for a world's fair, and it remained after its permit's expiration despite the controversy and the city's countless detractors.

ABOVE
Visiting Montreal's Biosphere in 2019 made our children's imagination connect some dots: Our middle daughter compared the structure to a dandelion out of the blue.

OPPOSITE
When conceiving the Dymaxion House, Buckminster Fuller dreamed of mass-producing precise homes as efficiently and affordably as Detroit had achieved with cars.

For one, said our youngest kid, the Biosphere didn't feel "point-less." It looked natural, one of our daughters agreed: "Of course it makes sense. Bouncy balls make sense. It's like a giant dandelion." We had found the ultimate image of Buckminster Fuller's protective enclosure. Only it wasn't our discovery but a deep, sometimes intuitive study the American polymath had himself pursued to come up with his super-lightweight and structurally sound domes.

Like Catalan architect Antoni Gaudí, known for his whimsical, nature-shaped modernist buildings in Barcelona, Fuller had sensed that some designs in nature, like the shape of some plants, were a testimony to the wisdom of evolution and a master class on how to carry weight efficiently. The "tensional integrity" of dandelions allowed them to keep their structural shape in strong winds despite their lightness, to accomplish the plant's dissemination goal.

In our quest to decipher Buckminster Fuller's experiments in housing, we left Montreal and kept driving down the mighty St. Lawrence River, the strategic entry point to reach the industrial heart of North America at the Great Lakes—and the access to the Mississippi Basin. The area's old industrial might had already vanished, yet we yearned to visit the Henry Ford Museum of American Innovation outside Detroit; our interest wasn't

OPPOSITE ABOVE
Danish engineer Martin
Manthorpe built the Dome
of Visions, a modern
Scandinavian home encased
within a geodesic dome,
to improve on the Nordic
climate, aid plant growth,
and offer extreme-weather
protection.

OPPOSITE BELOW
At a time of increasingly strict
regulations for home energy
performance, Manthorpe sees
the design as an alternative to
ultra-thick walls.

ABOVE
Originally designed for
Montreal's Expo 67, the
US pavilion's dome by
Buckminster Fuller sought to
blend science, sustainability,
and ingenuity.

cars but one man's dream to manufacture homes with the precision and convenience of cars or appliances. Right away, we spotted Buckminster Fuller's round, metal-clad Dymaxion House from afar.

The designer and futurist began working on the design in the 1920s by drawing a lightweight, prefab home that could be flat-packed and shipped worldwide. Any resemblance with Airstreams wasn't a coincidence, as recreational vehicles and prefabricated homes experimented with the strength and aerodynamics of modern airplane fuselages.

The Dymaxion ("dynamic maximum tension") was a concept of the times and included both a home and a car resembling future vans, such as the iconic Volkswagen T1. Lightweight and sturdy, it was made of aluminum and Plexiglas, weighing only 3,000 pounds (1,360 kilograms), less than many cars from the same era.

The self-enclosed services around the core of the circular layout required little maintenance, whereas the structure could be heated and cooled with natural ventilation, thanks to a vent opening on the dome's oculus. But, despite the early expectations, Fuller's circular prefab was never mass-produced. We will never know whether its aerodynamic design could have prevented widespread damages across the disaster-prone Mississippi Basin.

More than four decades after Fuller's death, geodesic domes remain among the boldest proposals to cheaply create self-enclosed environments capable of maintaining a controlled atmosphere to help regulate weather and air pollution and speed up plant growth. However, even though the time seems to have come to experiment with self-enclosed environments to regulate climate, air quality, or garden productivity, only a handful of homes accomplish the promises envisioned by pioneers such as Bucky Fuller.

A Danish team led by Kristoffer Tejlgaard and Benny Jepsen created the Dome of Visions a few years ago, a computer numerical control (CNC) cut wooden home inside a self-enclosed geodesic dome that acts as a greenhouse. The dome serves as the controlled "outside." When we visited this experimental dwelling in Copenhagen back in 2015, its climate-controlled interior seemed to emulate at a small scale what the Earth's atmosphere accomplishes with our planet.

Charles Sacilotto was inspired to build a house-in-a-greenhouse through his relationship with architect Bengt Warne, who began designing the first naturhus (nature house) in 1976.

J ust a few hours by car from the temporary place the experimental Dome of Visions had occupied in Denmark, we visited a family outside Stockholm, Sweden, that had successfully wrapped their home inside a greenhouse, reducing their energy bills—and environmental impact.

Despite the low average temperature in the area in the wintertime, what Marie Granmar and Charles Sacilotto experienced inside their greenhouse-wrapped wooden home was dramatically different: "For example, at the end of January, it can be -2 degrees Celsius outside, and it can be 15 to 20 degrees Celsius upstairs."

Both homes, the Danish Dome of Visions and the Swedish family greenhouse home, had a Scandinavian appeal, and their climatic principles reminded us of other idealistic structures created to benefit from the sun while preventing excess radiation. In the high desert of the American Southwest near Taos, New Mexico, a community of idealists had created what they called Earthships, self-sustained homes half-buried into the arid environment.

In winter, their glass facade gathers the sun's energy to heat their interior and grow food, staying at a constant temperature cooler than the outside during summer. Their design has evolved through trial, error, and adaptation from a design by architect Michael Reynolds in the 1970s; with their back buried against the ground, their Space Western aesthetic conceals a round design that uses postindustrial waste (old car tires, glass bottles, soda cans) in several different technical and aesthetic applications. Buckminster Fuller's ideas keep inspiring those experimenting with self-reliance in isolated areas defined by extreme weather.

Retired volleyball player Tom Duke had shown us the Earthship community in Taos a few years back, and we revisited once again amid the coronavirus pandemic, this time to interview sustainable construction consultant Deborah Binder on what had changed over the years in the design. The models, she told us, had gotten more efficient and affordable, an evolution expected in fields as apparently divergent as microprocessor density, industrial production, and productivity.

ABOVE LEFT
More than two decades ago, Tom Duke had just finished the pro volleyball circuit when he bought a bit of land with his wife and began to build a tiny Earthship the size of a storage shed, which evolved later as the family grew.

ABOVE RIGHT
On the desert mesa of New Mexico, miles from the nearest town of Taos, *Star Wars*–like shelters rise from the earth, half-buried and covered in adobe, called Earthships.

Their Space Western aesthetic conceals a round design that uses postindustrial waste (old car tires, glass bottles, soda cans).

OVERLEAF
Loyal to their principle of earth sheltering for climate and indoor gardening, Earthships have improved over the years; newer builds capture more energy, water, and food at a lower cost.

When we first visited the
Earthship Community
outside Taos, New Mexico,
in the summer of 2014, our
children were very young.
They had a blast in the high
desert fairylands.

Avoiding destruction, or entropic acceleration, has not yet reached mainstream status, but DIYers worldwide are testing their Mad Max-style housing prototypes against climate disaster to create their own version of beauty—only this time it's out of postindustrial leftovers. Some people interested in tinkering and boundless experimentation in the digital and industrial worlds are trying to improve construction and affect how dwellings take care of people and places. Influenced by informal desert gatherings such as pop-up villages for land sailing, the Burning Man festival, or their own compass, they turn industrial-era materials or leftovers into solar punk or postapocalyptic dwellings, from rusted shipping container dwellings to modern homes made from car and other postindustrial scraps.

Back in the early aughts, we realized the use of shipping containers in construction didn't make much sense to some architects, structural engineers, and urbanists: Could a commoditized, standardized, almost antivernacular metal box that had been created to ship goods overseas be reused as a building block? Soon, shipping container homes, offices, and even apartment buildings began having their enthusiasts, but also detractors.

Yet innovation is accelerating in the low end of the housing market, where victims of destitution, young idealists, entrepreneurs, technology,

and traditional real estate investors try to find common ground to translate experimentation into realistic, often creative proposals to improve housing.

Today, many people might struggle to differentiate between some of the experimental homes and communities in these pages and video game or movie sets, such as the shipping-container town of *Ready Player One*. In retrospect, we feel lucky to be among the catalyzers of this change in public perception—whether of innovative housing or adaptive ways to live in a challenging future. What was once controversial and "very experimental" is now mainstream, from accessory dwelling units (also known as "granny units") to no-VOC materials, to unconventional designs, modularity, and many more factors.

To some, building with salvaged materials and postindustrial "leftovers" is the path to integrate the past into one area's vernacular and urban regeneration. Others use low-impact materials instead of cement, while many innovators have gone full circle, acknowledging that wood, a renewable material, can help build simple cabins, as well as airports and skyscrapers.

All of which gives us inspiration, as we document the changes yet to come. Until now, we could not easily show our audience the thinking behind our endeavors or the connections we find as we work—and how this influences our experience and our family. We hope this book does that, and we also hope that it both challenges and delights you by offering a look inside the many places friends all over the world call home.

ABOVE LEFT
How do we want to live? Is it necessary to use toxic materials and build sanitation everywhere, or can natural materials and composting toilets also be a part of the future?

ABOVE
The so-called diseases of
civilization trigger immune
responses and allergies
due to, in part, poor indoor
air quality. Natural homes
recover the porosity of
homes from the past with
the efficiency of modern
homes.

ACKNOWLEDGMENTS

This book wouldn't have been possible without the many friends and acquaintances that have tuned in to our website *faircompanies and Kirsten's YouTube channel; consider this book a present to you first and foremost, and hopefully a window (or a door, or a portal) you can open once in a while so you can peek out or go outside and take a breath with us.

Secondly, our thanks also go to the people who opened their lives and homes, which they cherish most, so we could share their inspiring stories in our work—this book included.

Finally, we want to address you, dear reader: If this book feels like a walk by our side near the woods outside your home, we'll have accomplished what we intended. Thoreau invited us to walk in the woods around a local pond not far from his hometown; taking his example, we want to introduce you to some of our friends, houses, and stories, which each one of you will complete with your own personal story and appreciation. You can share it with us if or when you think it's time. :)

Special thanks to our very-exigent-but-kind agent, Kristin van Ogtrop, for her work to make this book happen; and to Shawna Mullen and Darilyn Carnes, editorial director and book designer at Abrams, respectively, for their wise, competent work and dear patience with us.

This adventure didn't only involve Kirsten and Nico: It was illuminated by three independent and wise copilots, our children Inés, Ximena, and Nicky, representatives of the new generations.

Finally, to the idealists and quixotic misfits that bring awe to the world so we can re-enchant it. You have us on your side.

ABOUT THE AUTHORS

Sixteen years ago, Kirsten Dirksen and Nicolás Boullosa founded *faircompanies and set out with a video camera, travelling the globe to understand the varied and surprising ways people can live in the modern world. On their YouTube channel—which now has over 1000 videos and nearly two million subscribers—they document the quirky, ambitious, solitary, enterprising, and moving.

Their path to YouTube fame has been as unexpected as the dwellings they discover. After graduating with a BA in economics from Harvard, Kirsten spent a decade filming pop culture for teen shows at NBC-San Francisco and Oprah-startup Oxygen Media, as well as working for Sundance and Shania Twain. The California native searched through Europe for secrets behind *The Da Vinci Code* novel for Discovery, and produced on-the-road films with bands for MTV. But it was on a trip to Spain to interview Javier Bardem for the Sundance Channel that she met Nicolás Boullosa, and a new chapter of her life began.

A native of Barcelona, Nicolás Boullosa was the editor in chief of the magazine *Digitalware*, director of several online publications, and an editor at *Playboy*. Nicolás is passionate about creating in-depth, non-partisan, quality digital content to improve public discourse on subjects that either threaten or improve well-being. He has written and translated several books with topics ranging from the fictionalized contact between Neanderthal and Sapiens groups in prehistoric Europe to the future of blockchain and web3. As a journalist and writer interested in photography and nature, he attended a program in free-market environmentalism at the Property and Environment Research Center (PERC) in Bozeman, Montana.

Soon after meeting, Kirsten and Nicolás launched *faircompanies, a website featuring videos that showcase their core values of sustainability and minimalism (both for them personally, and for the planet).

Today, Kirsten and Nicolás spend most of their time in Europe and the U.S., filming and editing for their YouTube channel, where viewers can see frequent cameos of the couple's three children.

CREDITS

All photos by Nicolás Boullosa and Kirsten Dirksen, except: p. 7, Ethan James Green for Vanity Fair Magazine; pp. 19-20, George Suyama; p. 38, Diana Lorence; pp. 53-55, Gary Zuker; pp. 56-57, 62-63, Wes Modes; pp. 74-76, Tas Careaga; p. 77 Below, Nerea Moreno; p. 78, Below, Tim Seggerman; pp. 86-89, Paul Cutting; p. 100, Above, Greg Parham; pp. 102-103, p. 104, Above, p. 105, Emmanuel Pauwels; pp. 132-133, Above Left, Simon English; pp. 160-161, Chris Tack; pp. 168-169, Jeff Sousa; pp. 170-171, Jenna Jonas; pp. 172-173, Sean Peng; p. 175, Top Right, Darren Bradley; p. 178, Paul Elkins; p.193, Above, Dan Schultz; p. 214, José Hevia; David Tapias; p.217, Above, p. 218, Below, p.219, p. 235, Top Right, Ty Cole; p. 226, Søren Aagaard

Editor: Shawna Mullen
Design Manager: Darilyn Lowe Carnes
Managing Editors: Annalea Manalili and Jodi Wong
Production Manager: Larry Pekarek

Library of Congress Control Number: 2024943579

ISBN: 978-1-4197-7189-7
eISBN: 979-8-88707-668-3

Printed and bound in China
10 9 8 7 6 5 4 3 2 1

Abrams books are available at special discounts when purchased in quantity for premiums and promotions as well as fundraising or educational use. Special editions can also be created to specification. For details, contact specialsales@abramsbooks.com or the address below.

Abrams® is a registered trademark of Harry N. Abrams, Inc.

ABRAMS The Art of Books
195 Broadway, New York, NY 10007
abramsbooks.com